Dear Nature and Art Enthusiast,

As you hold this book in your hands, you are not merely acquiring a set of coloring pages; you are about to embark on a unique journey of self-discovery and tranquility. "Magnificent Wild Animals" is more than just a coloring book; it is an invitation to explore the beauty of the animal kingdom while getting lost in the mesmerizing shapes of carefully designed mandalas.

We hope that each stroke of your pen or brush is an act of kindness to yourself, a well-deserved pause in the daily chaos. Allow each color to be an expression of your emotions, a celebration of the nature that surrounds us. This book is a sacred space for your creativity to flourish and your mind to find peace.

May the hours spent with "Magnificent Wild Animals" be moments of self-care, where stress dissipates, and the joy of creation takes over. By coloring these mandalas, you are not merely filling in blank spaces; you are adding life and energy to every detail.

May this work be more than just a book; may it be a companion guiding you to a state of serenity, a constant source of inspiration. Appreciate each page as a gift you deserve, and may each chosen color be a reminder of your own uniqueness and beauty.

Thank you for choosing "Magnificent Wild Animals." We look forward to seeing the wonders you will create and the stories each stroke will tell. May this book bring joy, peace, and a touch of magic to your coloring journey!

With warmth,

Jorge Pereira
2024

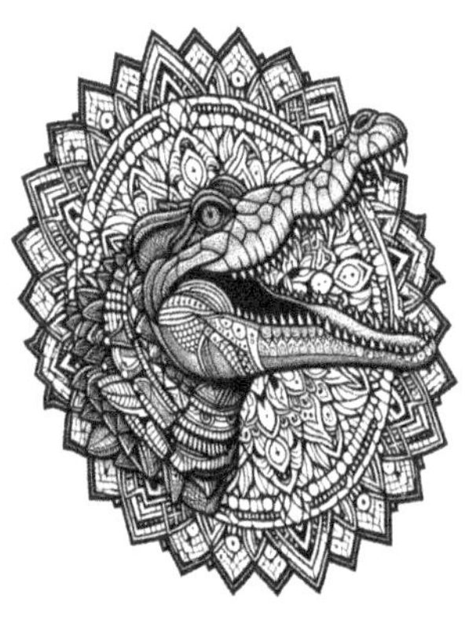
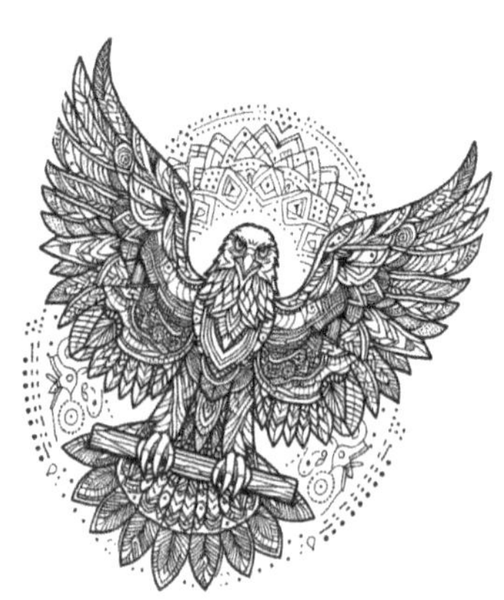

This Book Belongs to.

____

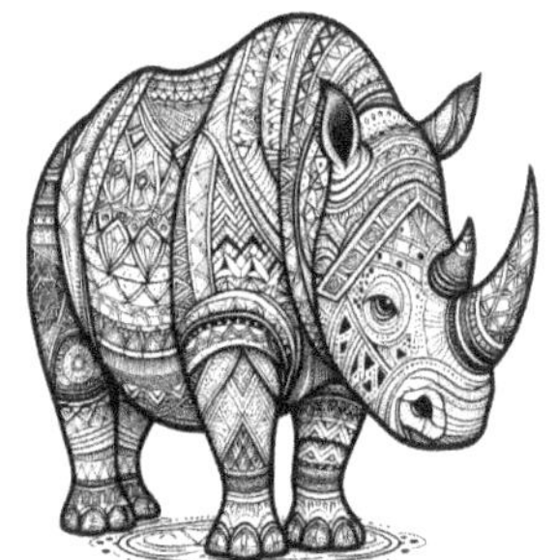
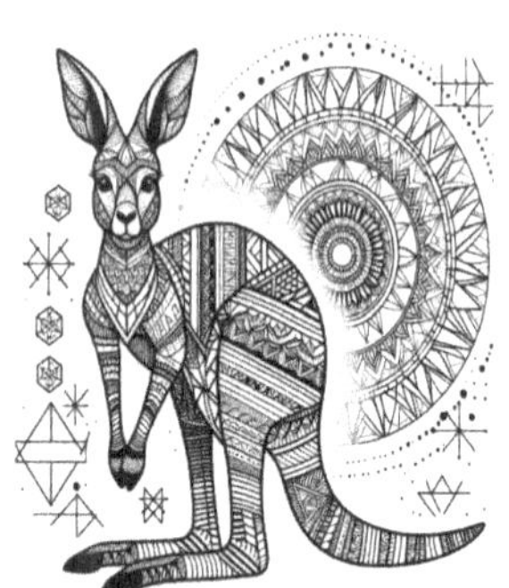

J.P.P.©

TEST COLOR PAGE

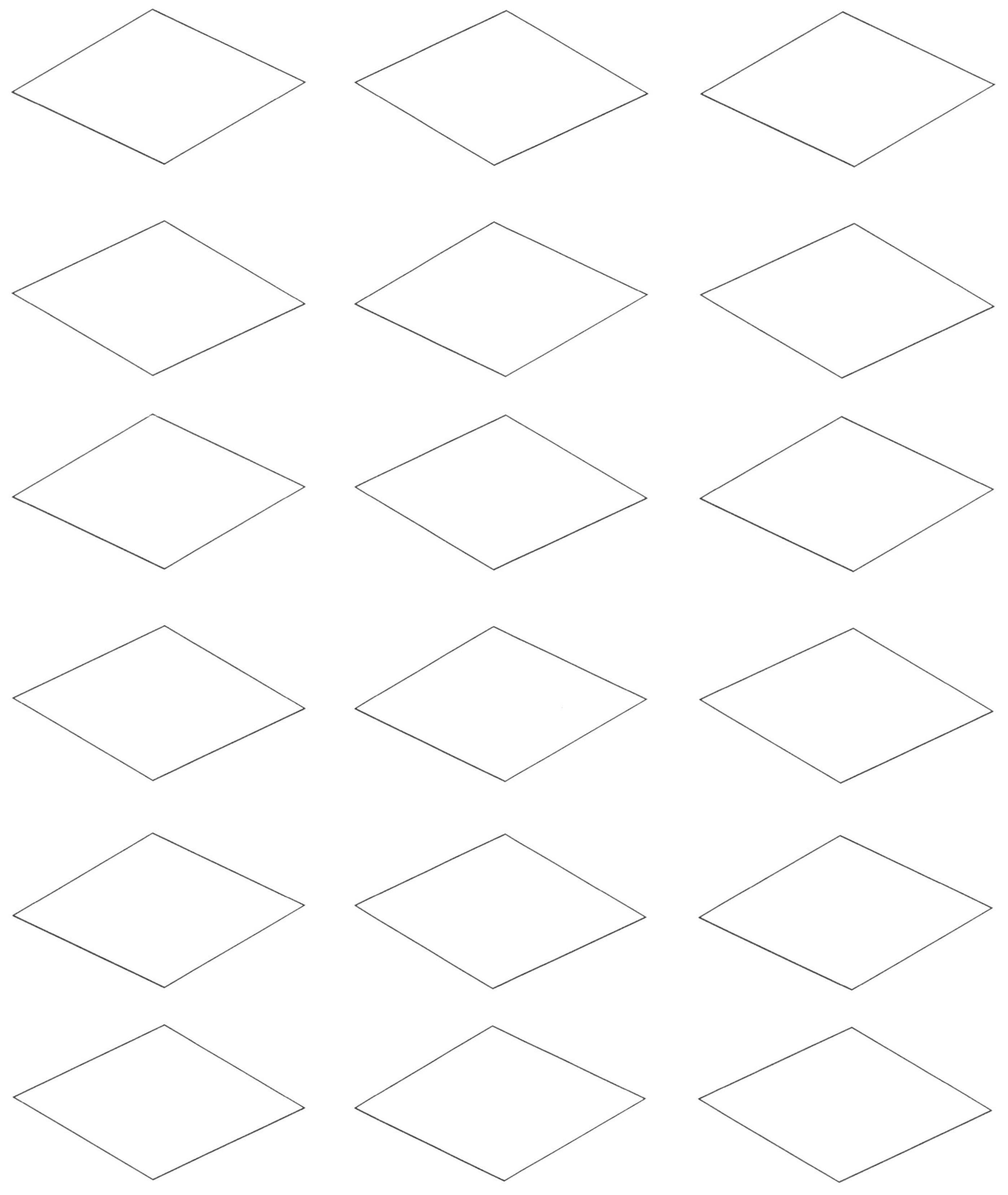

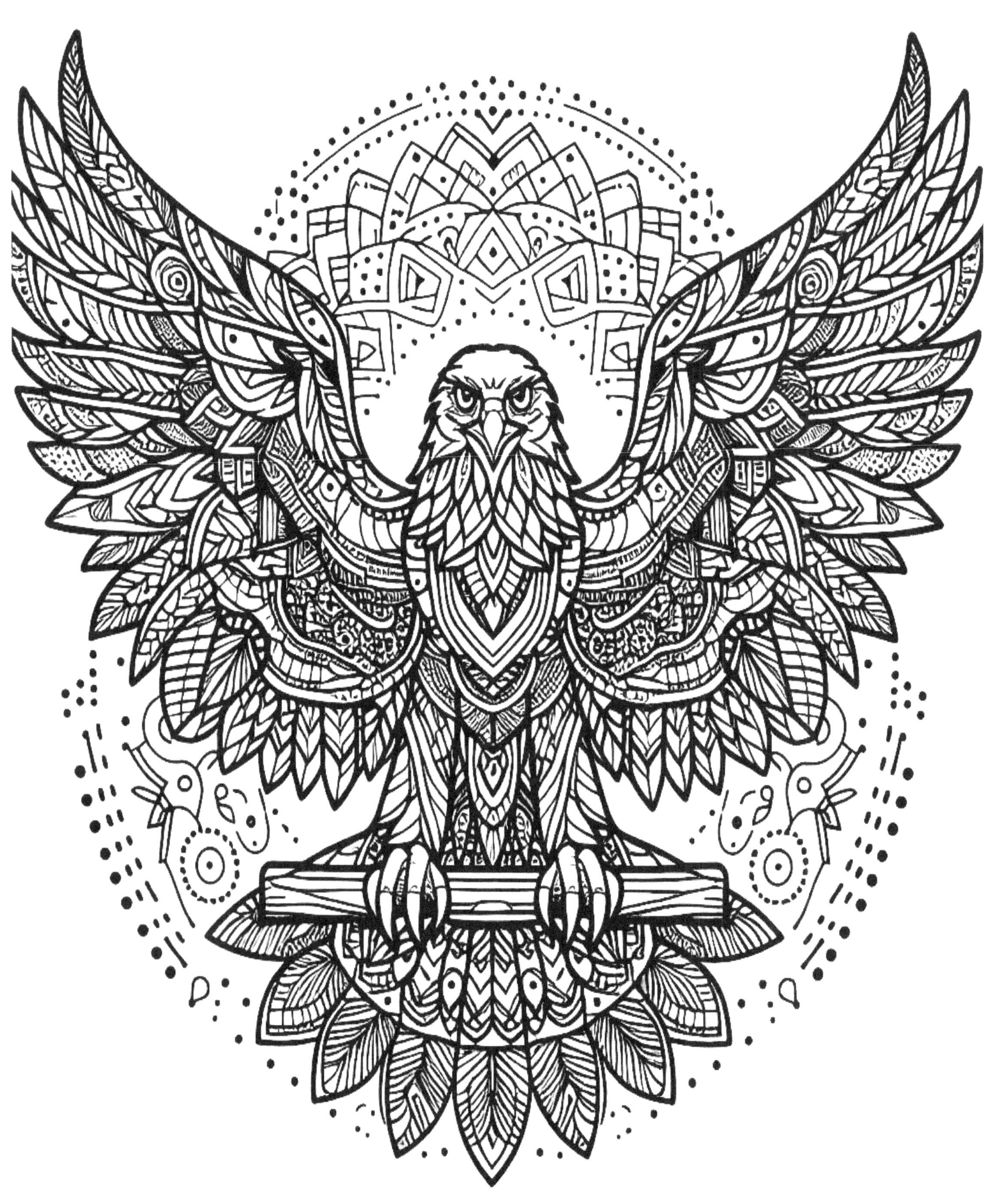

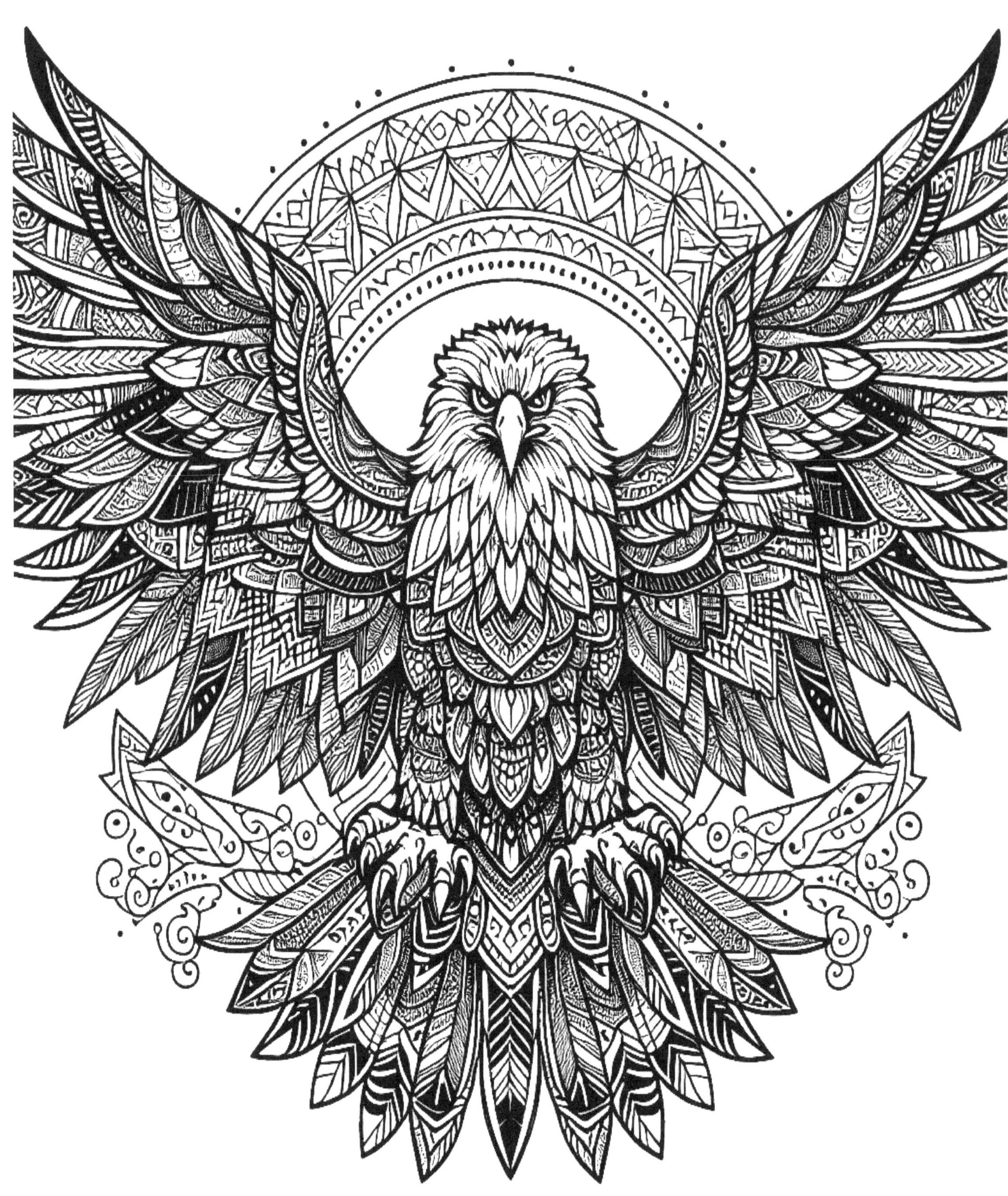

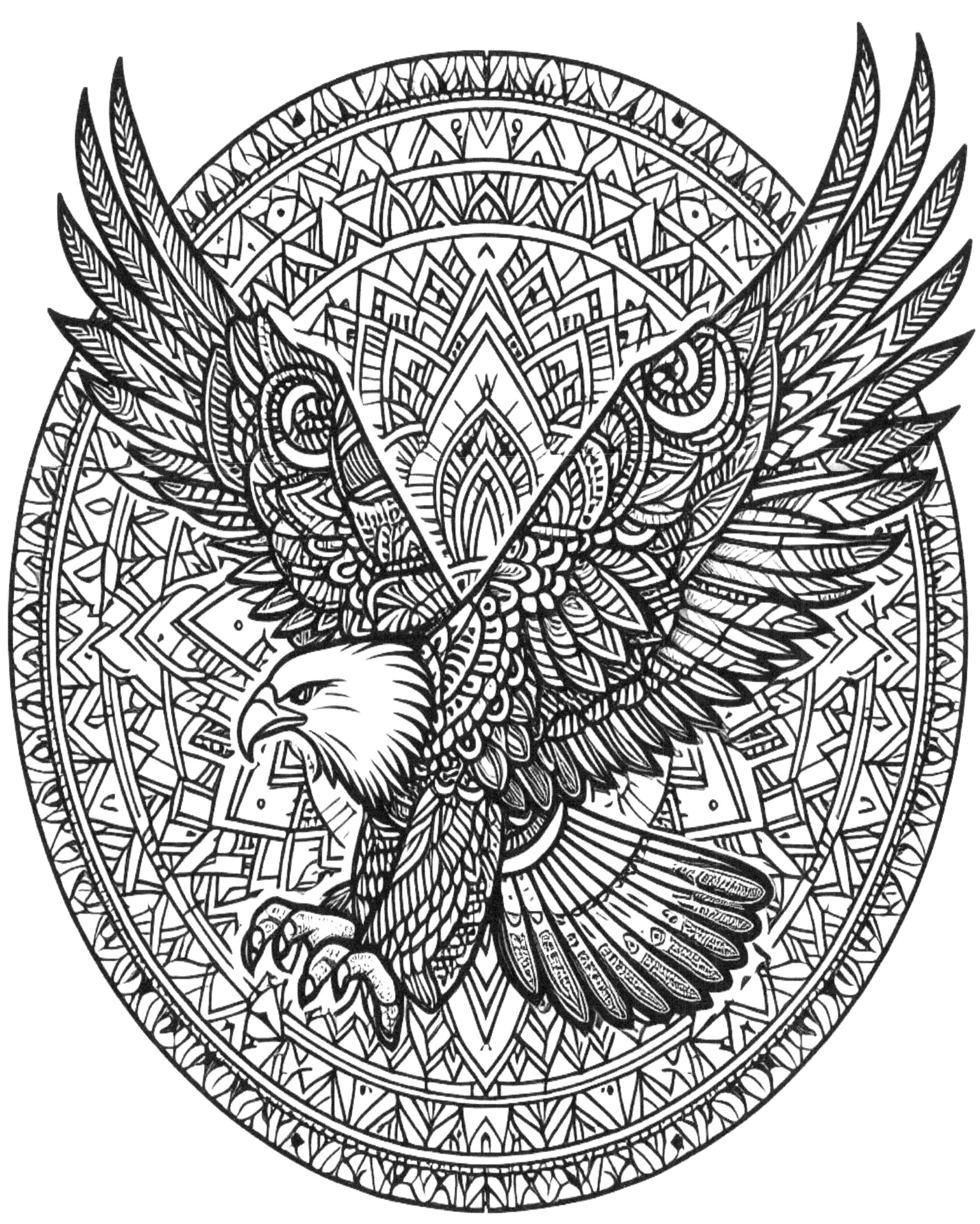

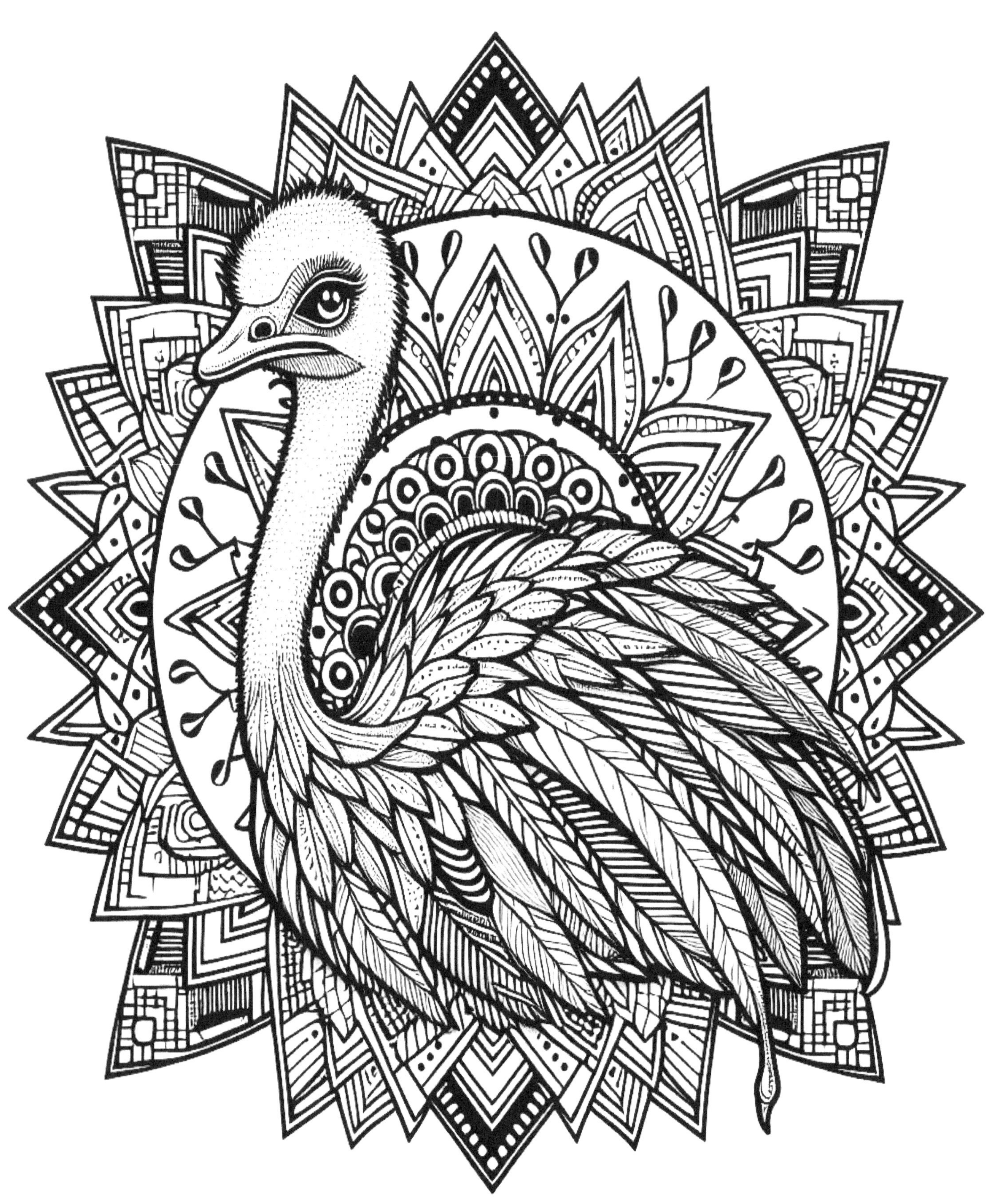

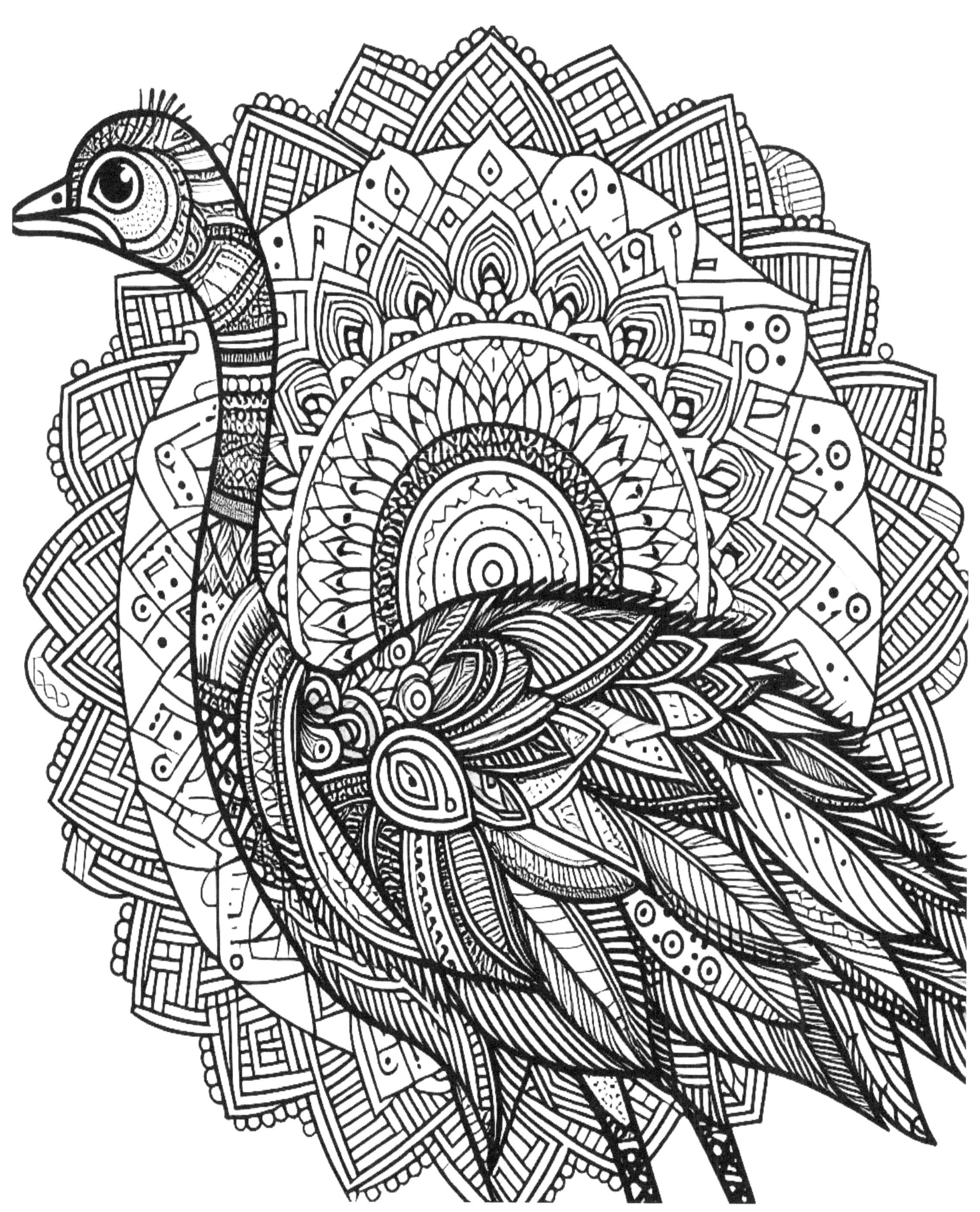

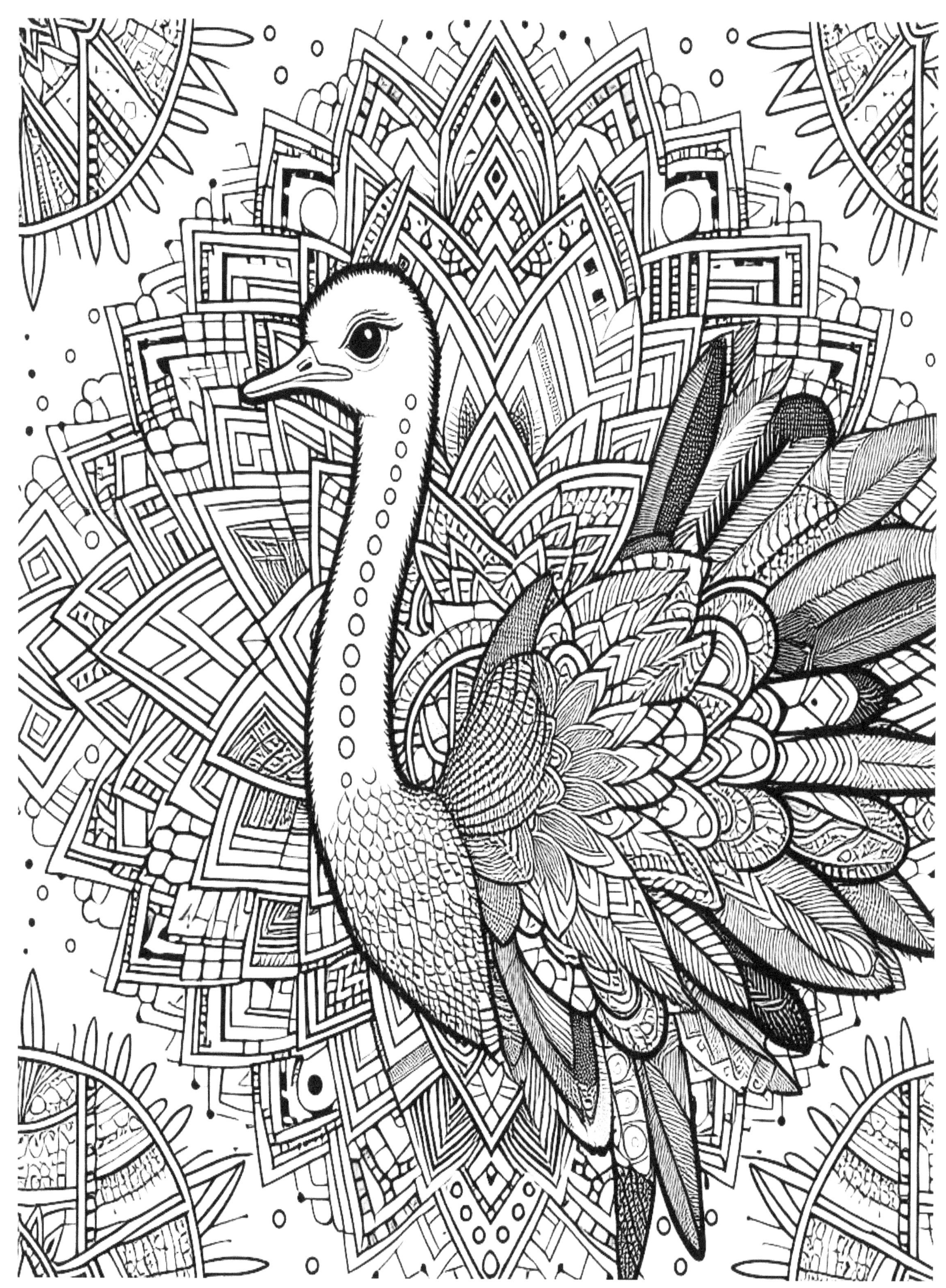

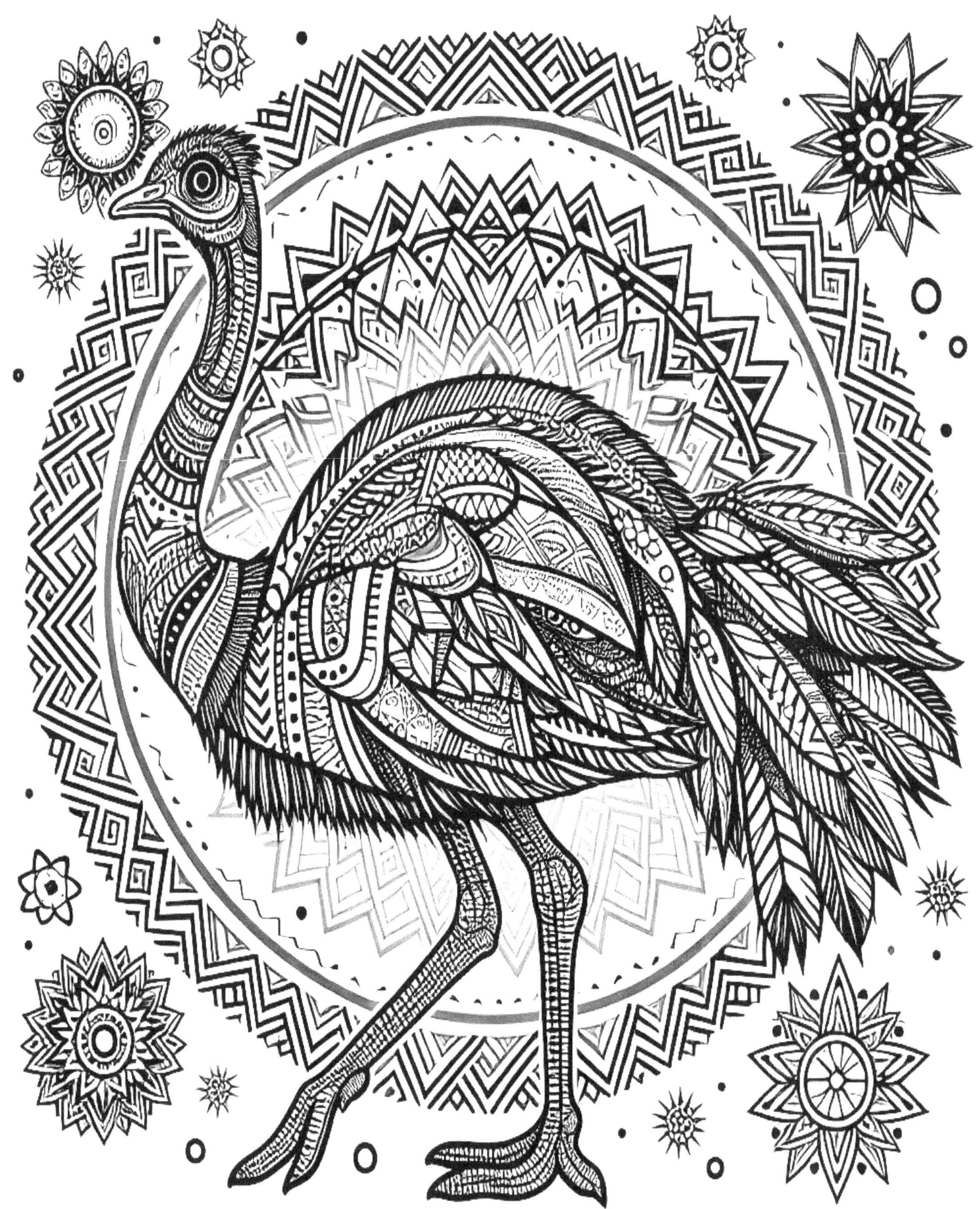

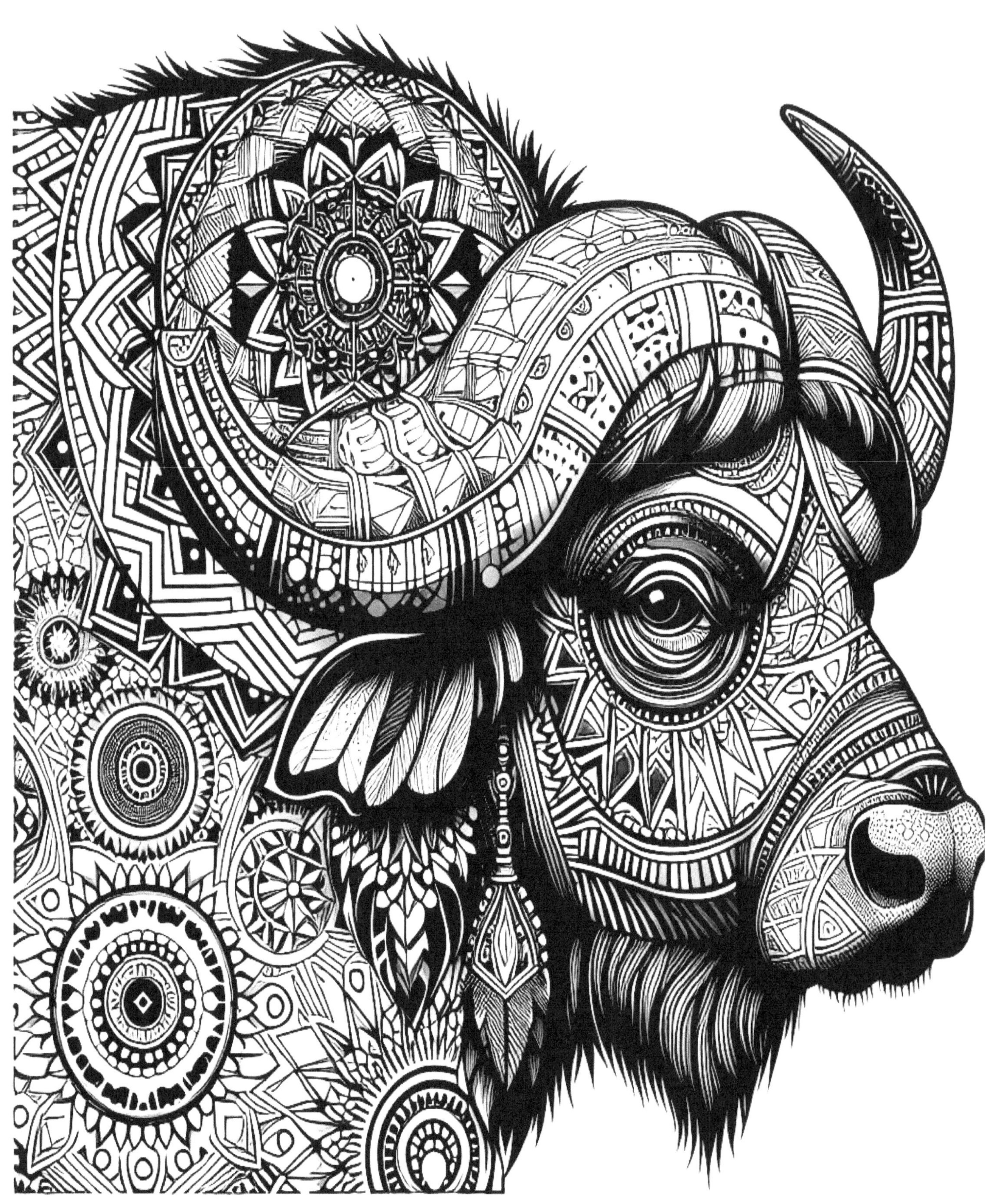

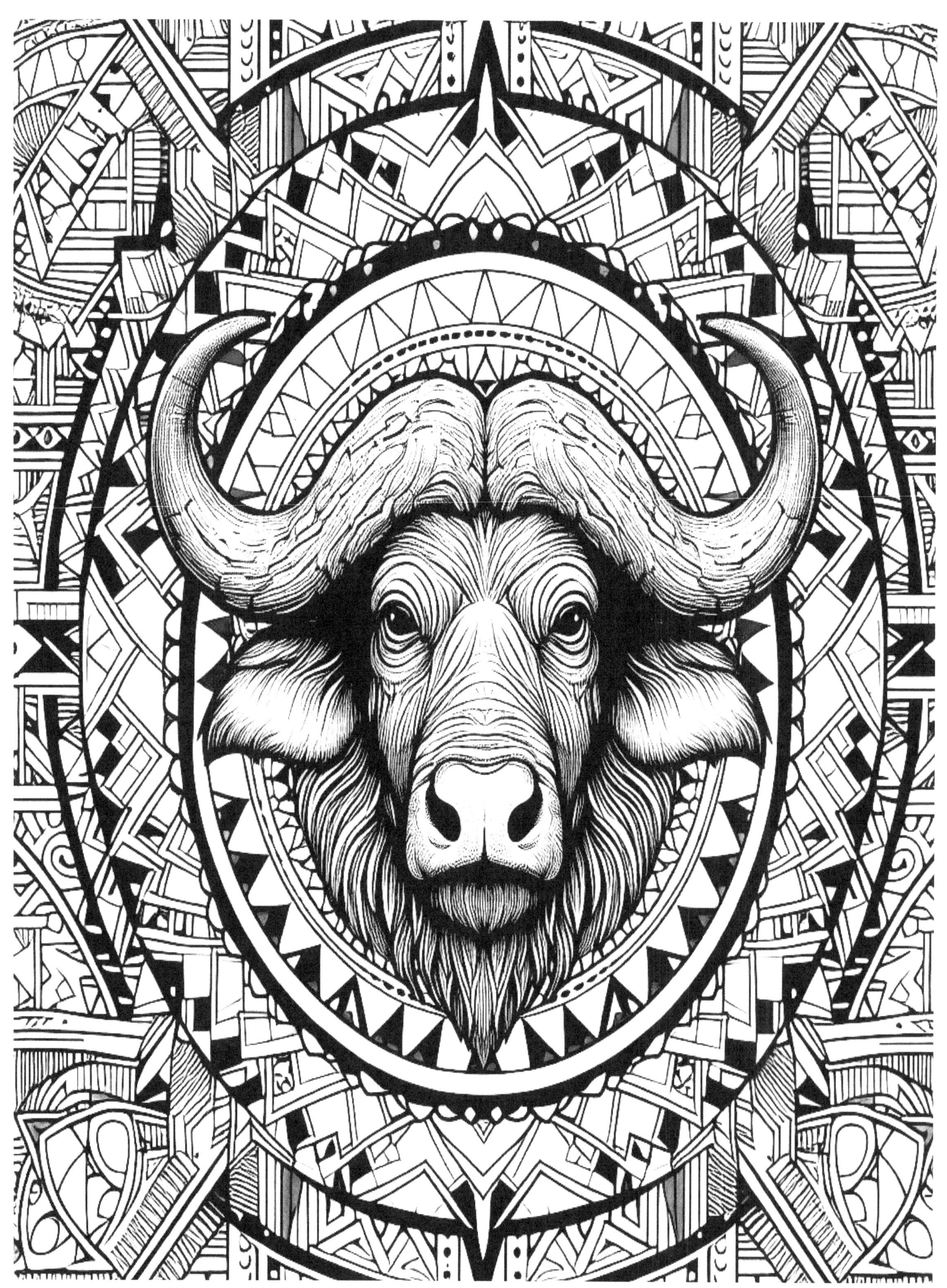

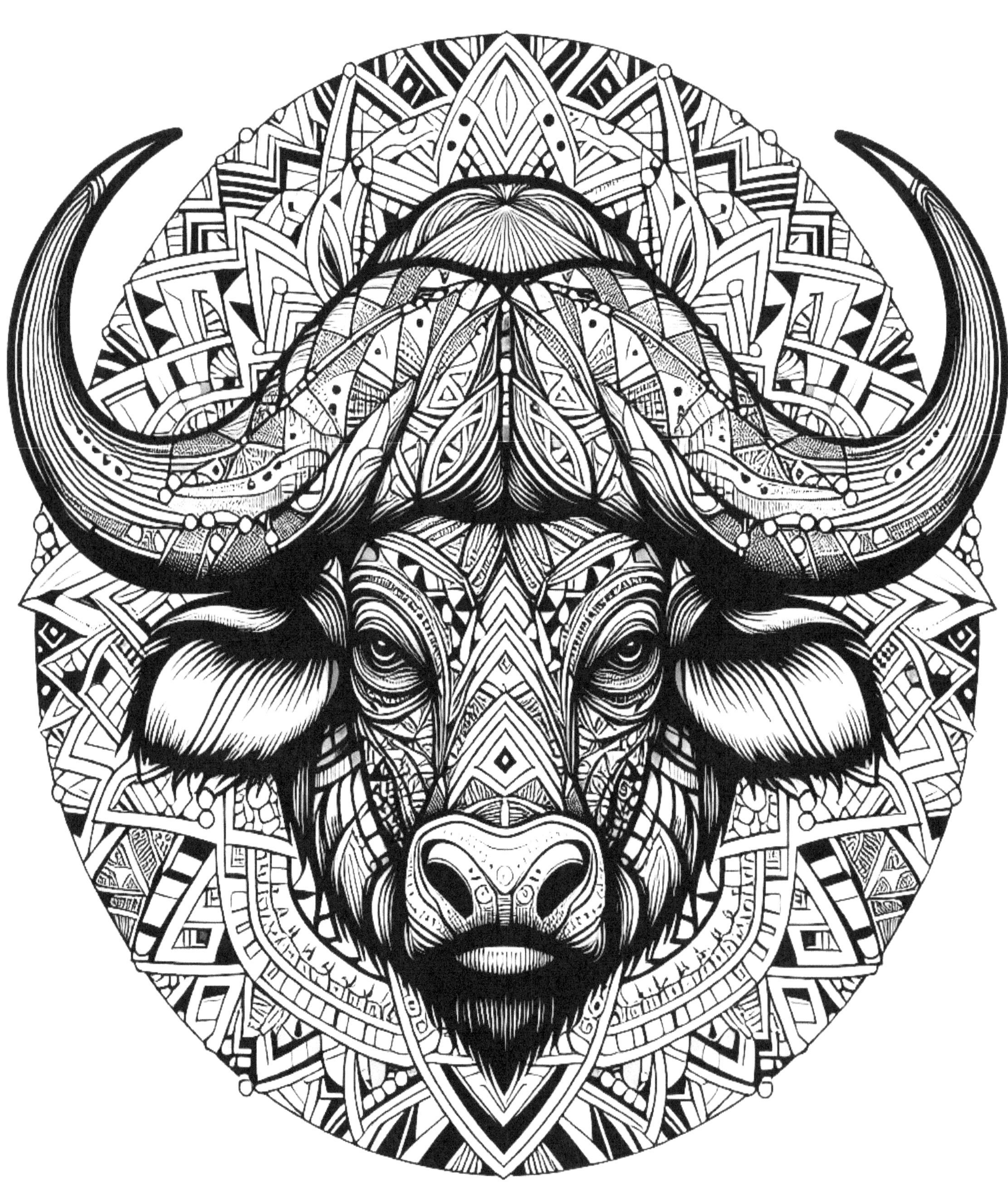

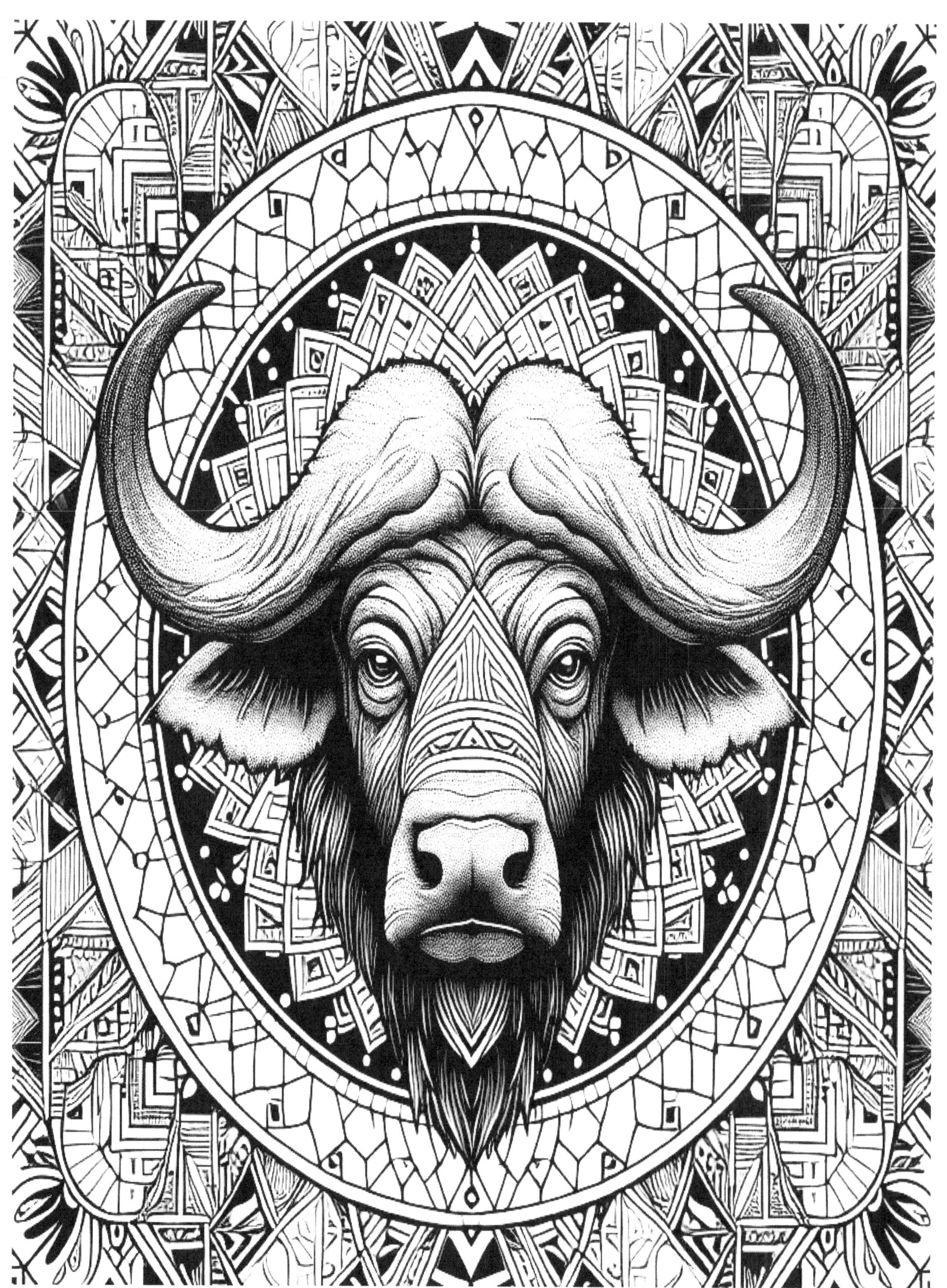

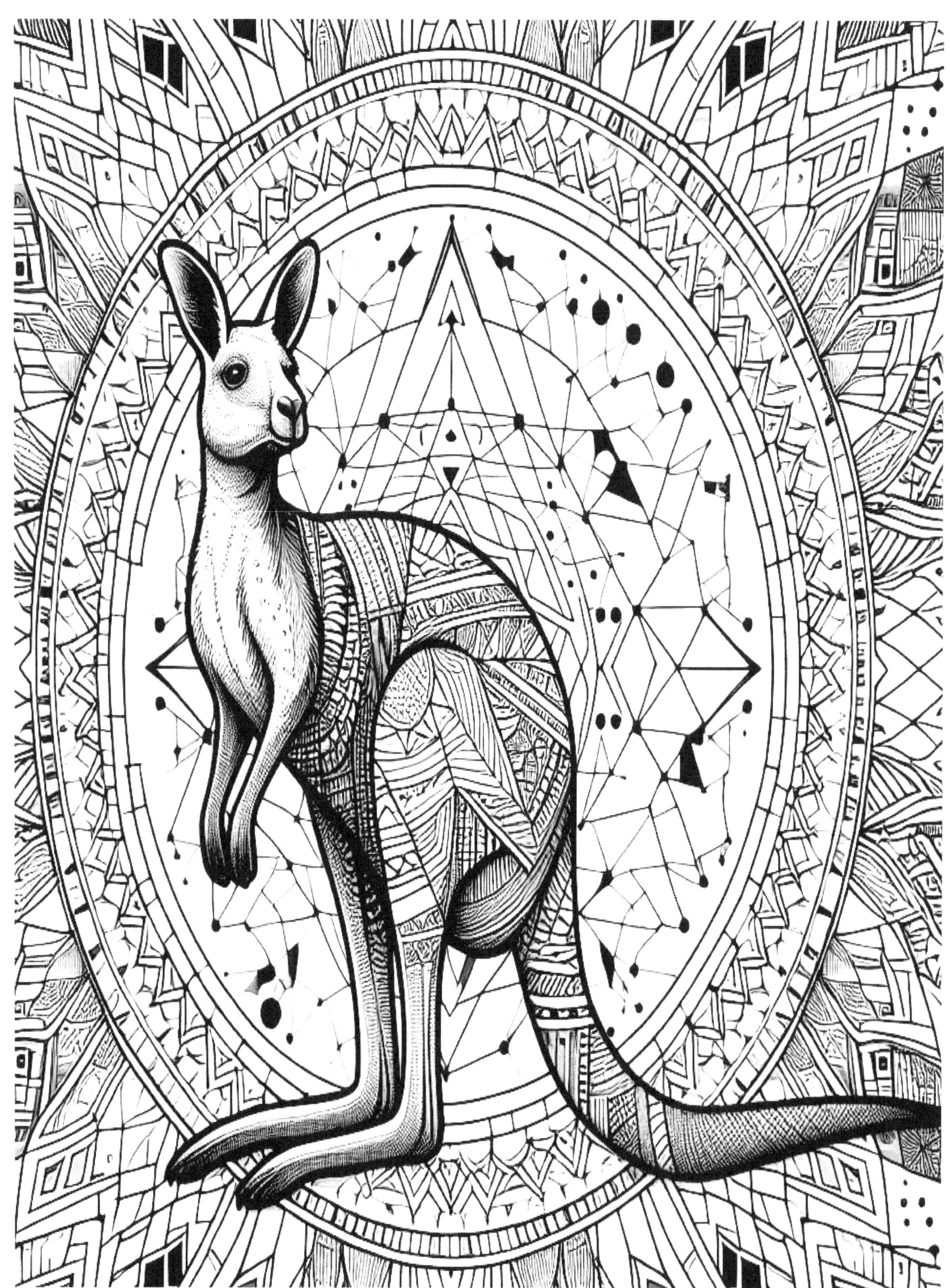

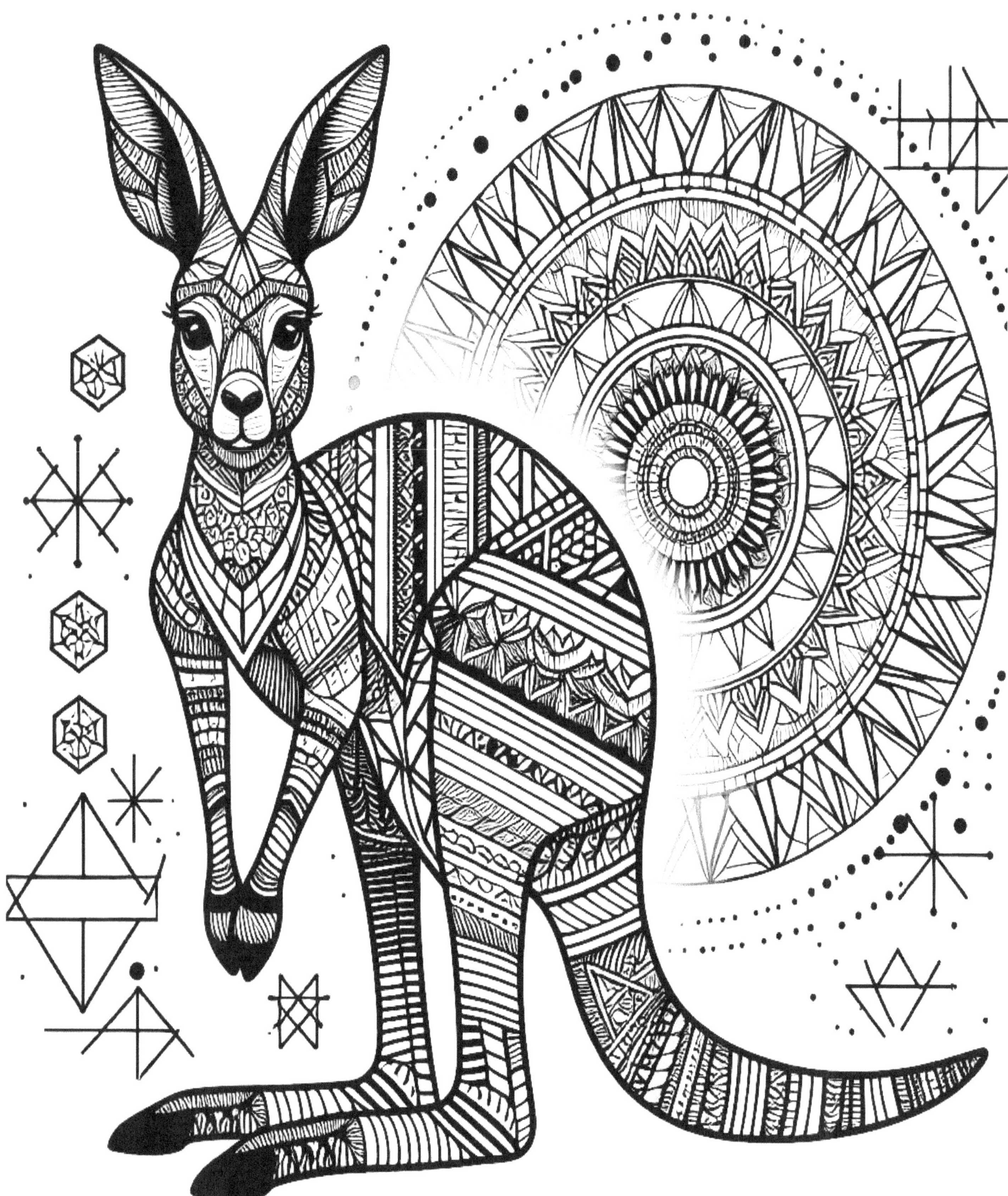

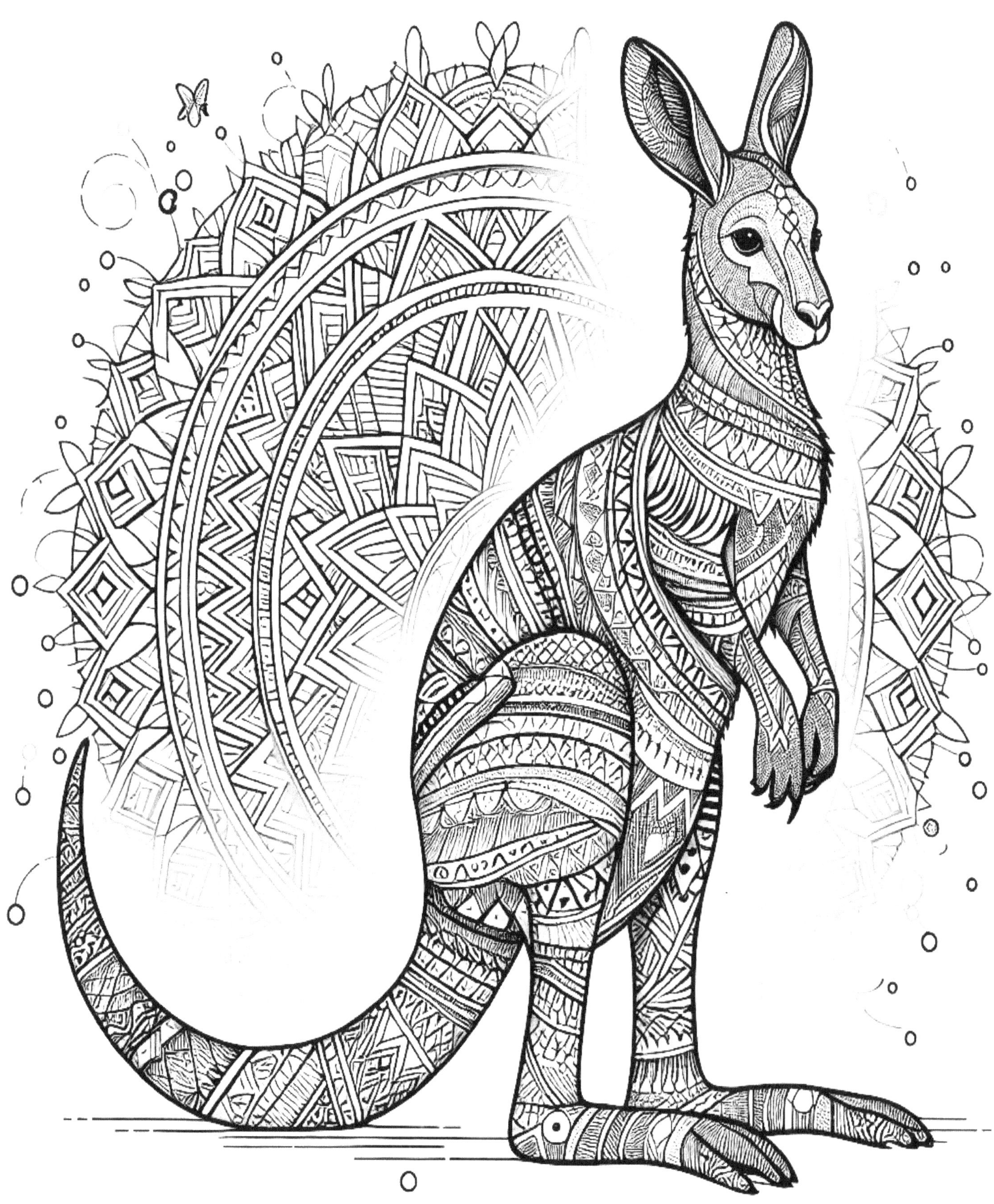

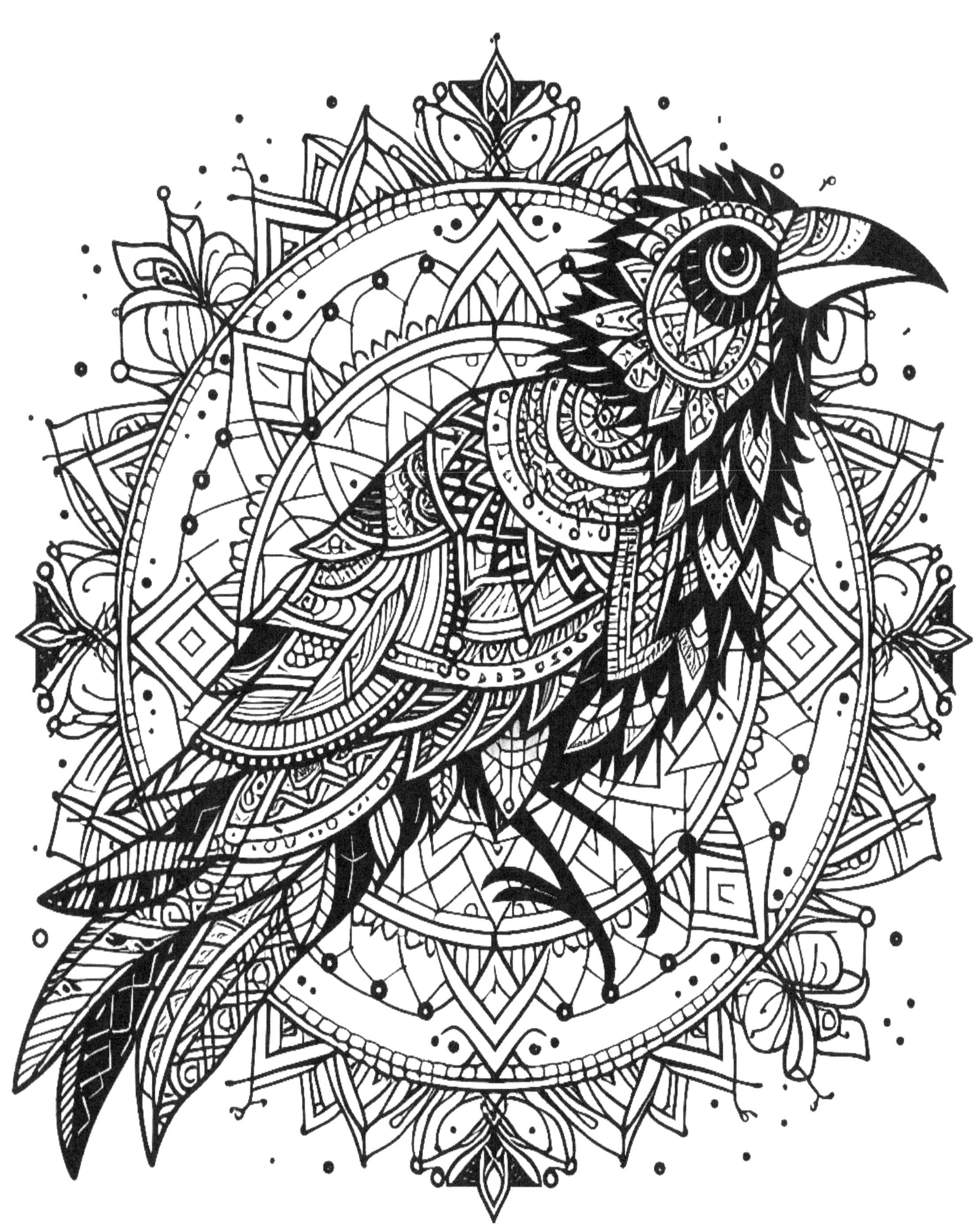

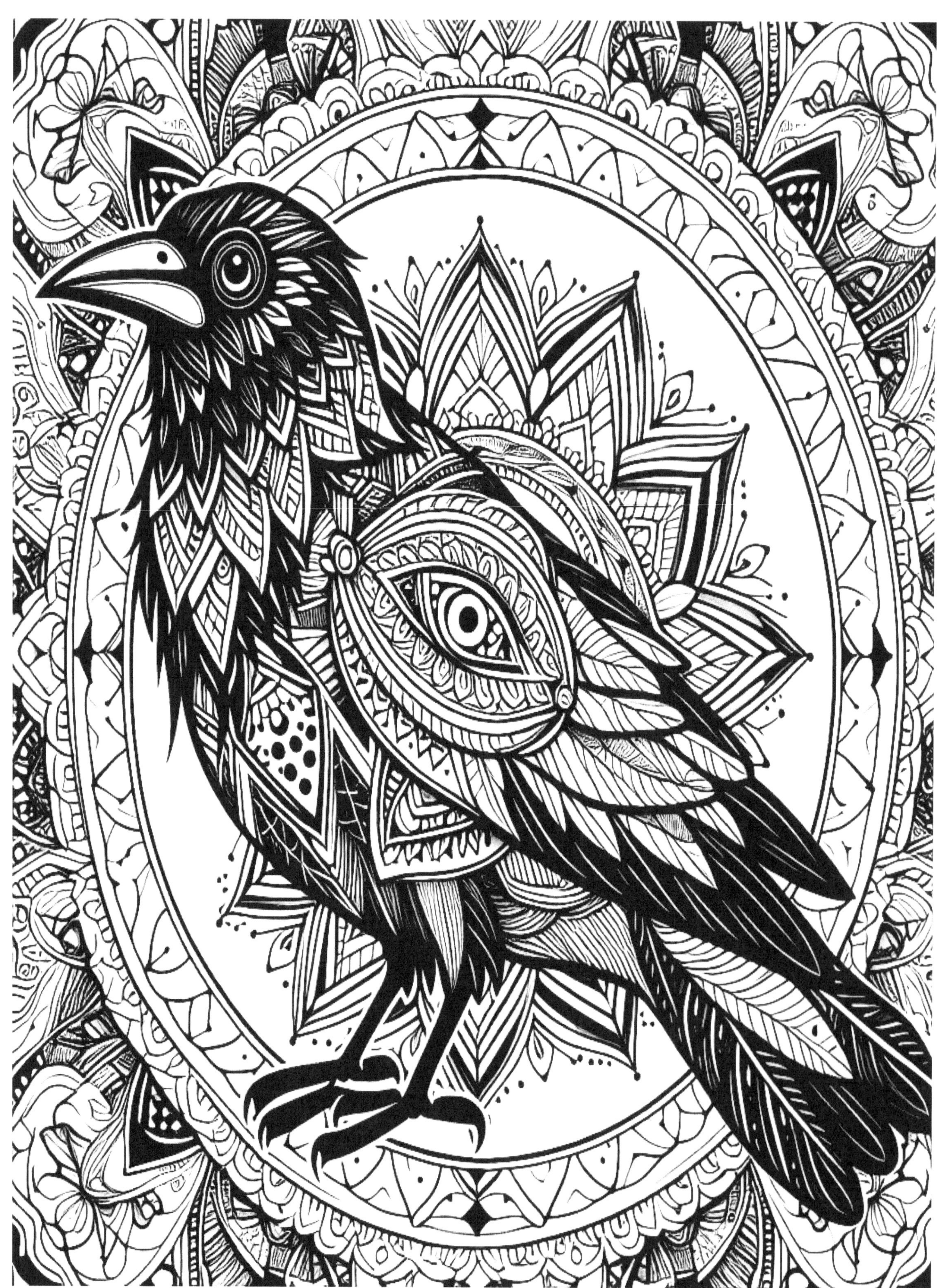

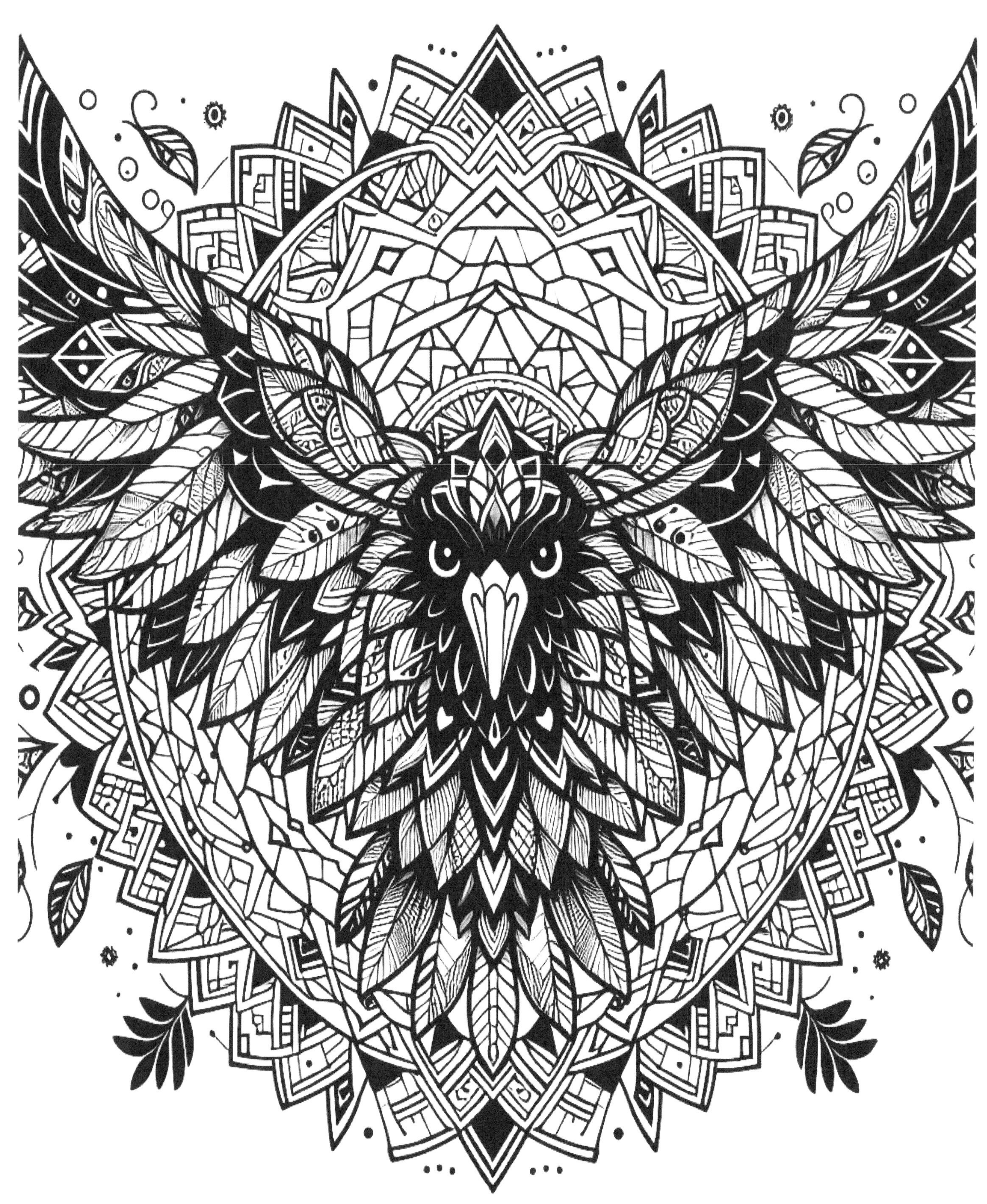

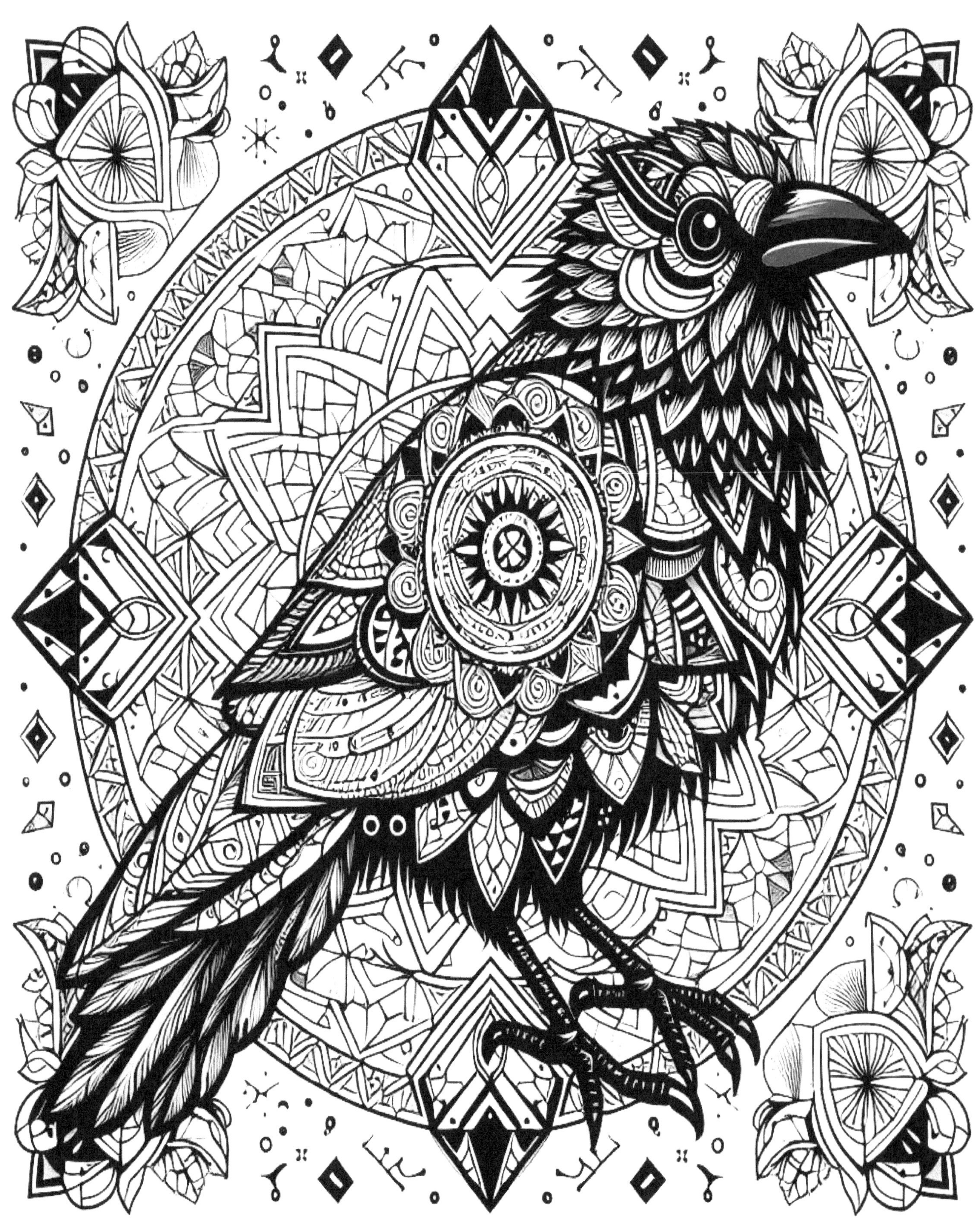

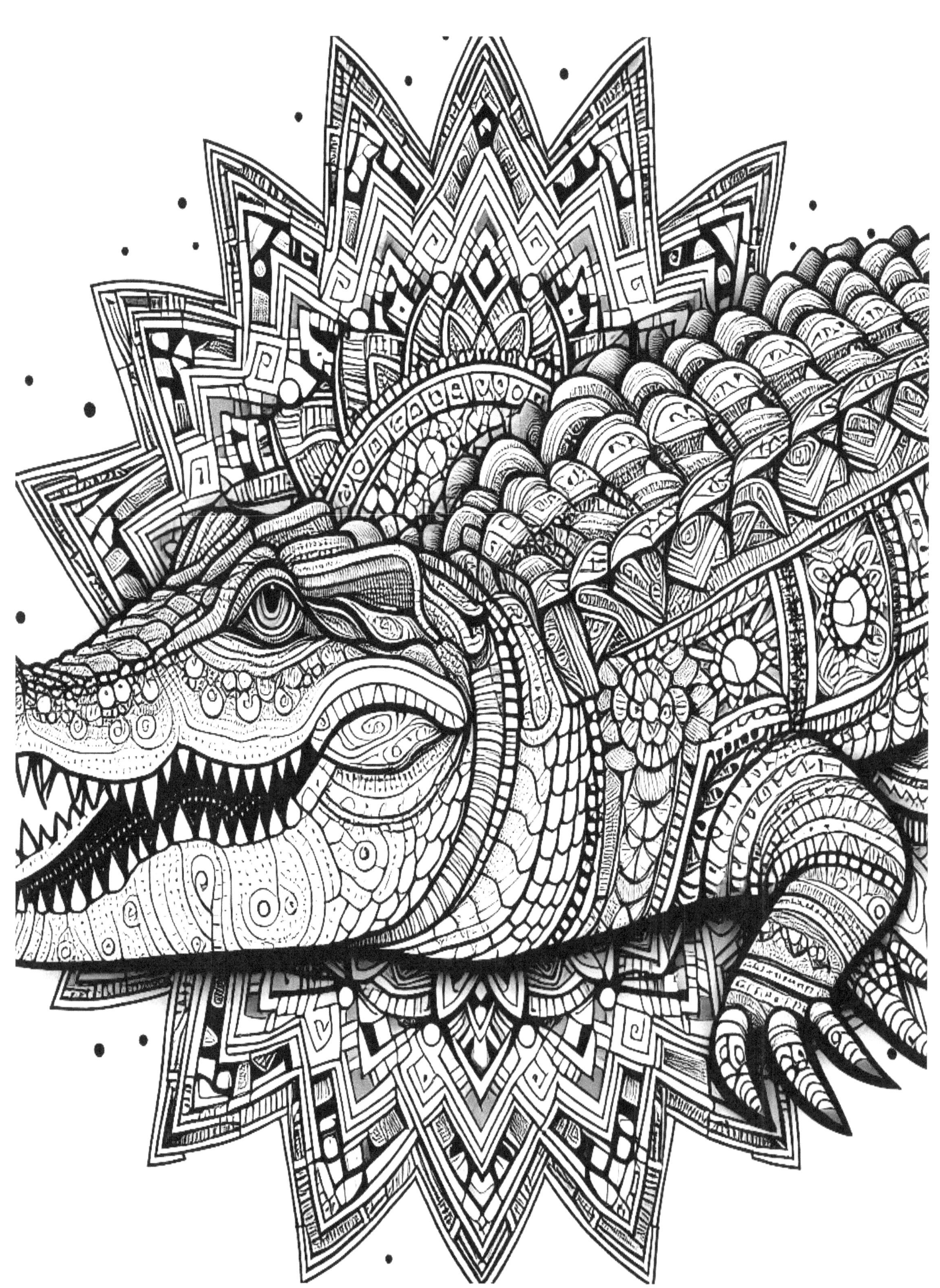

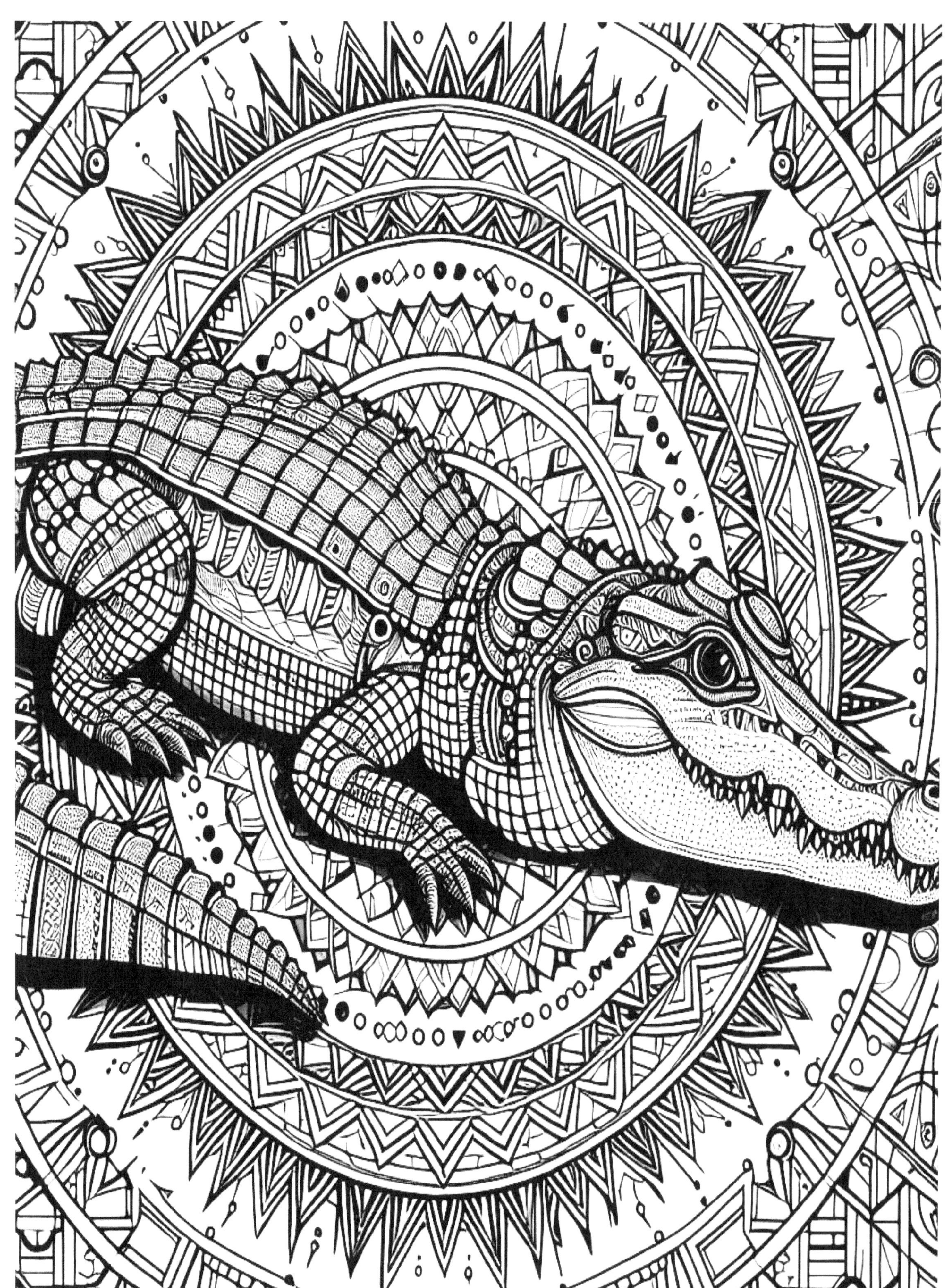

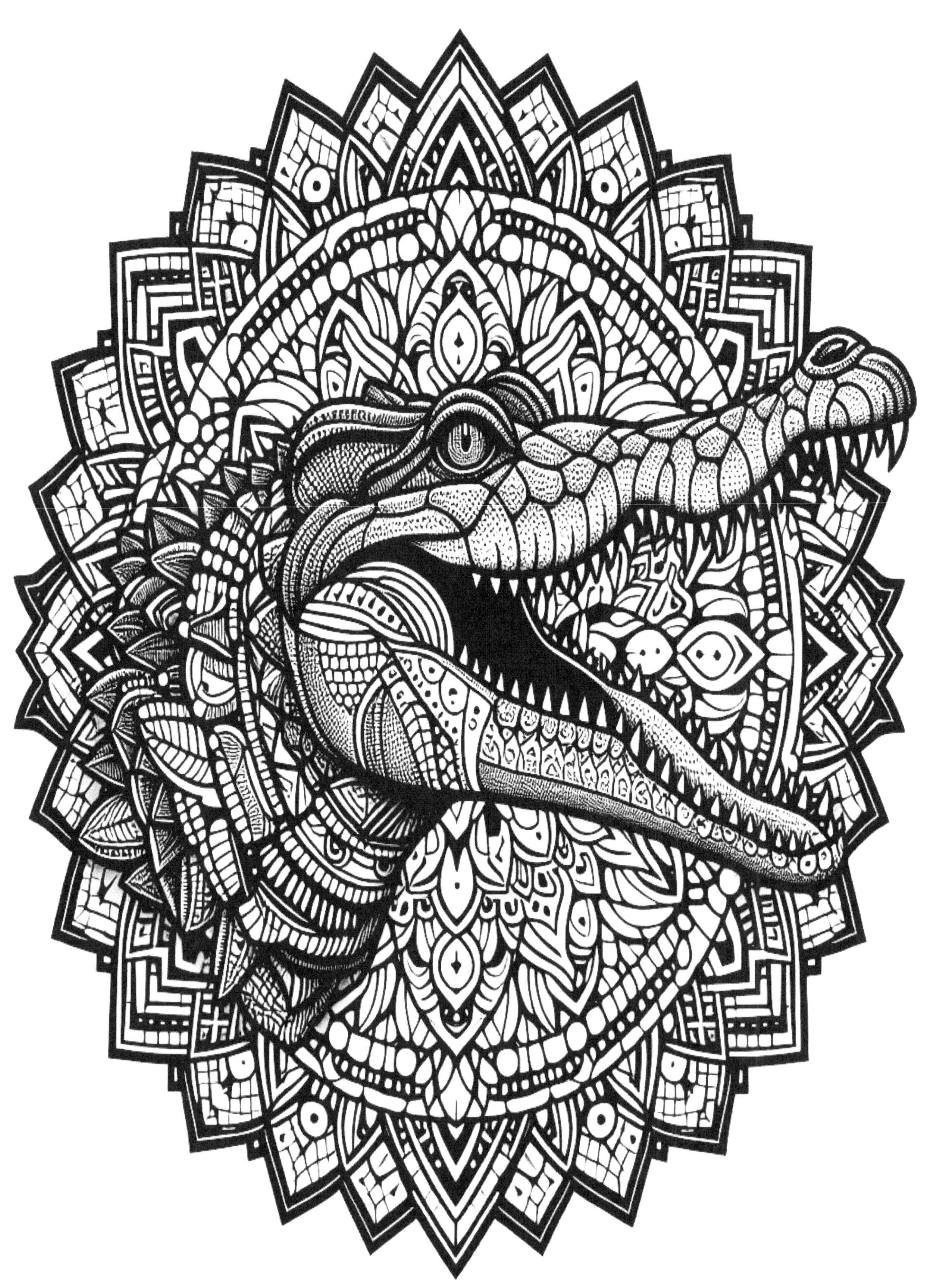

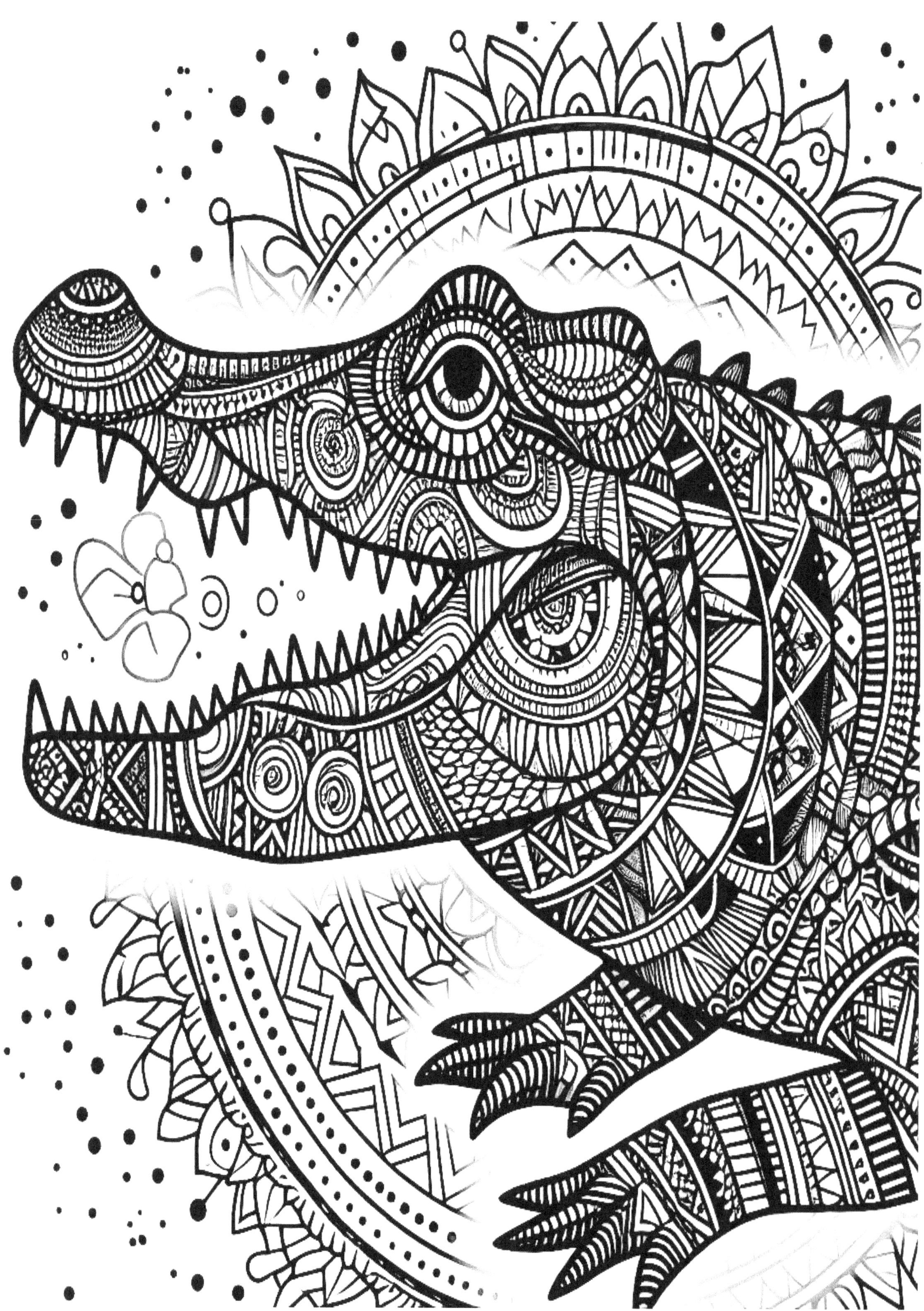

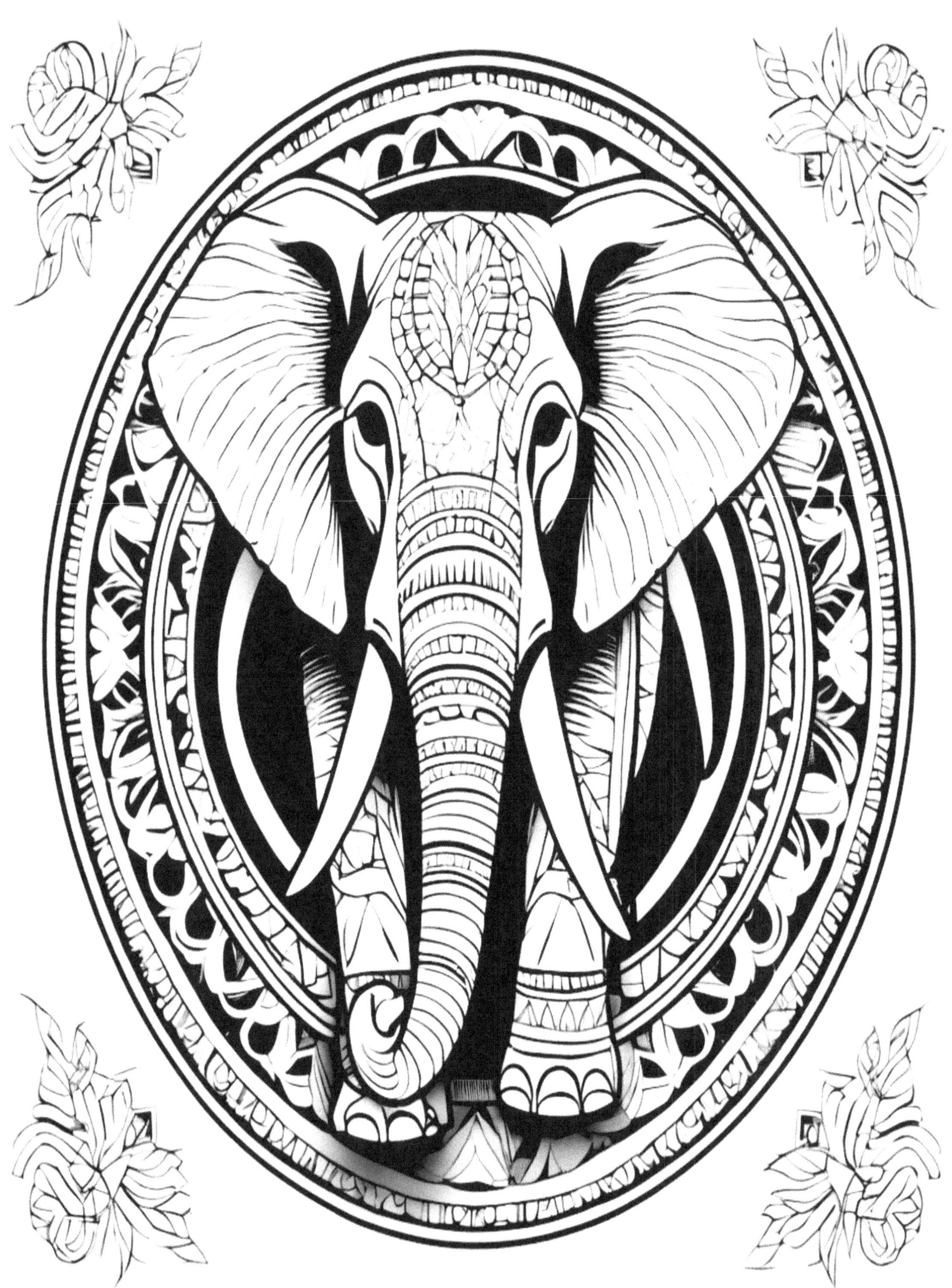

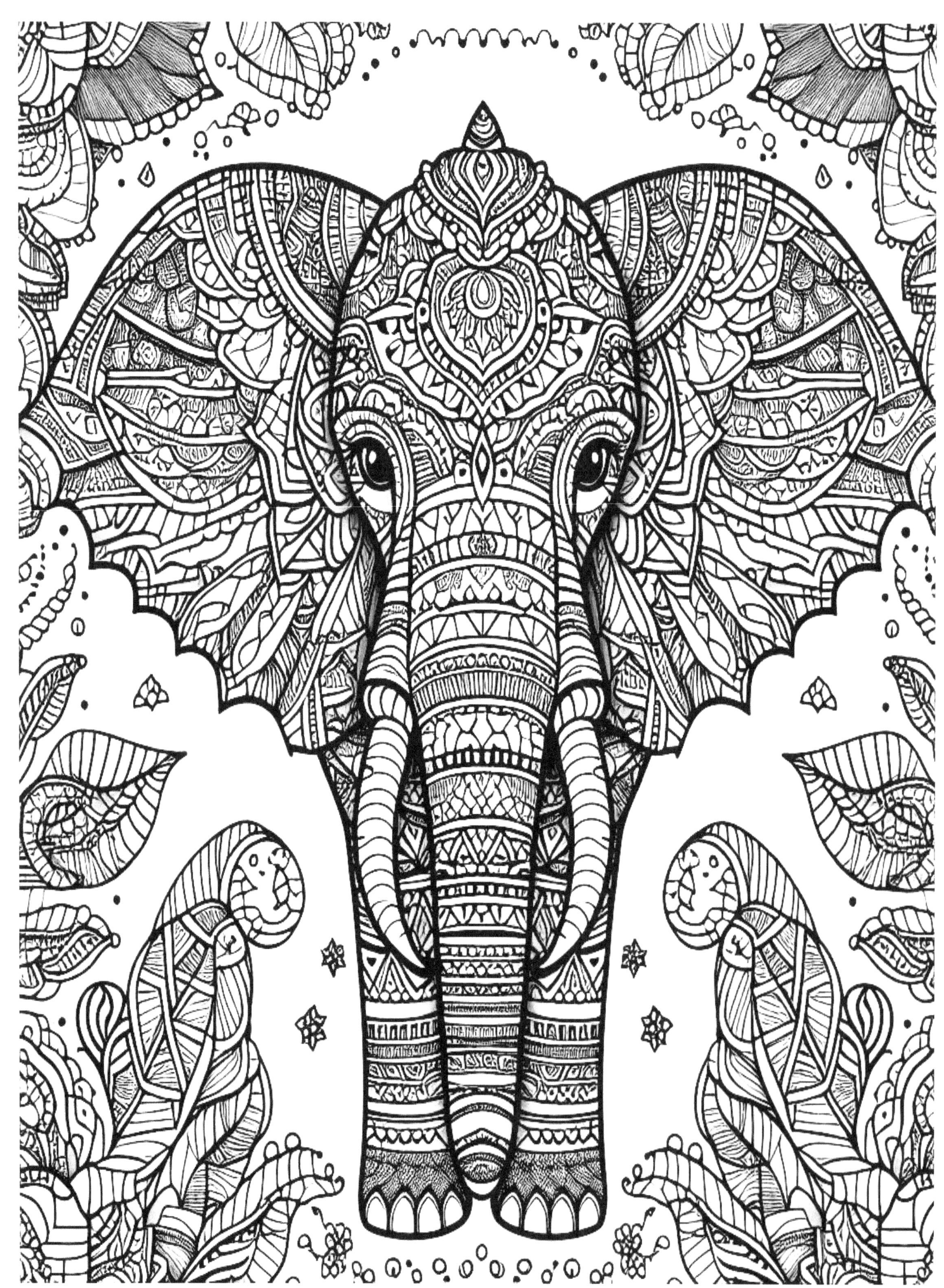

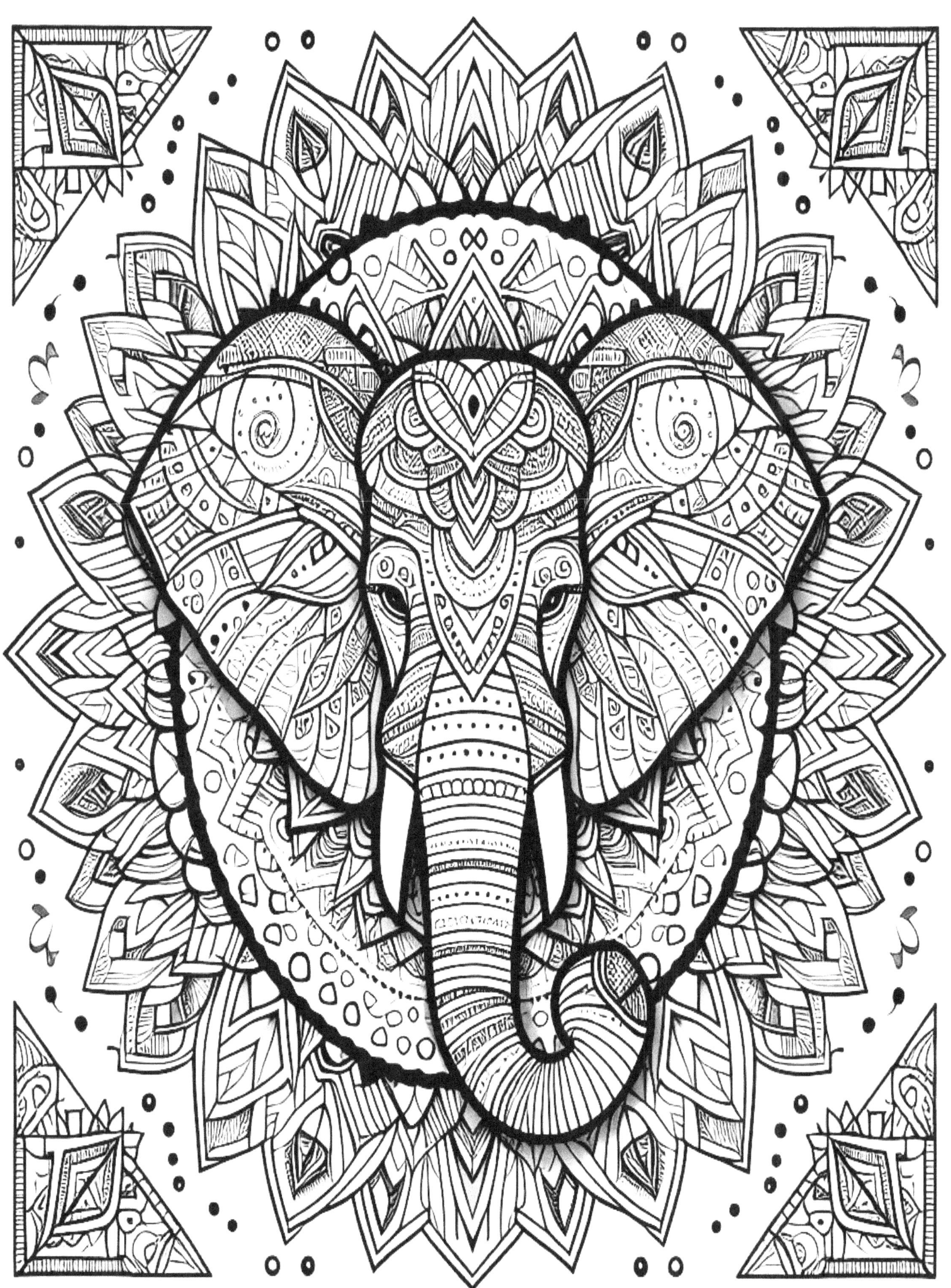

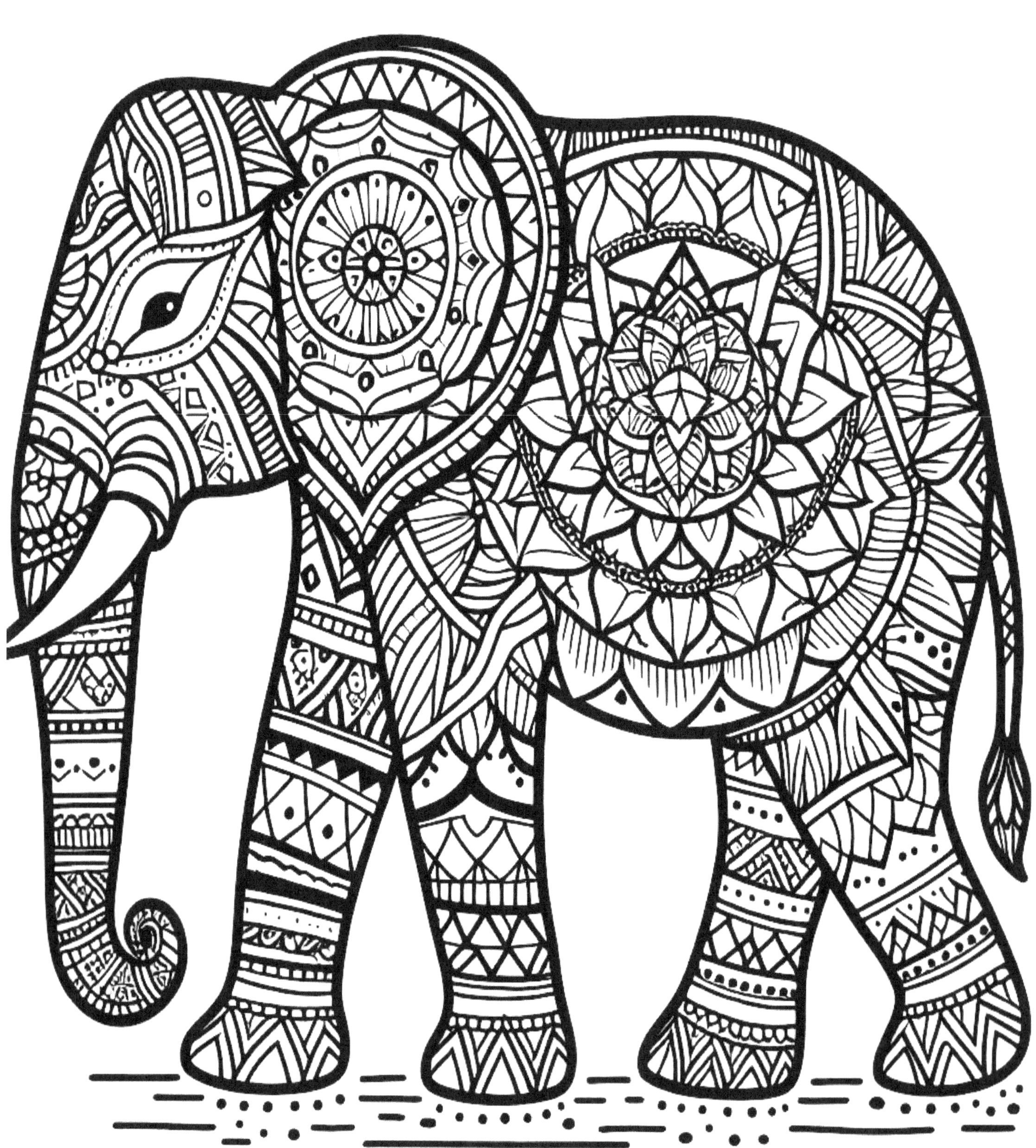

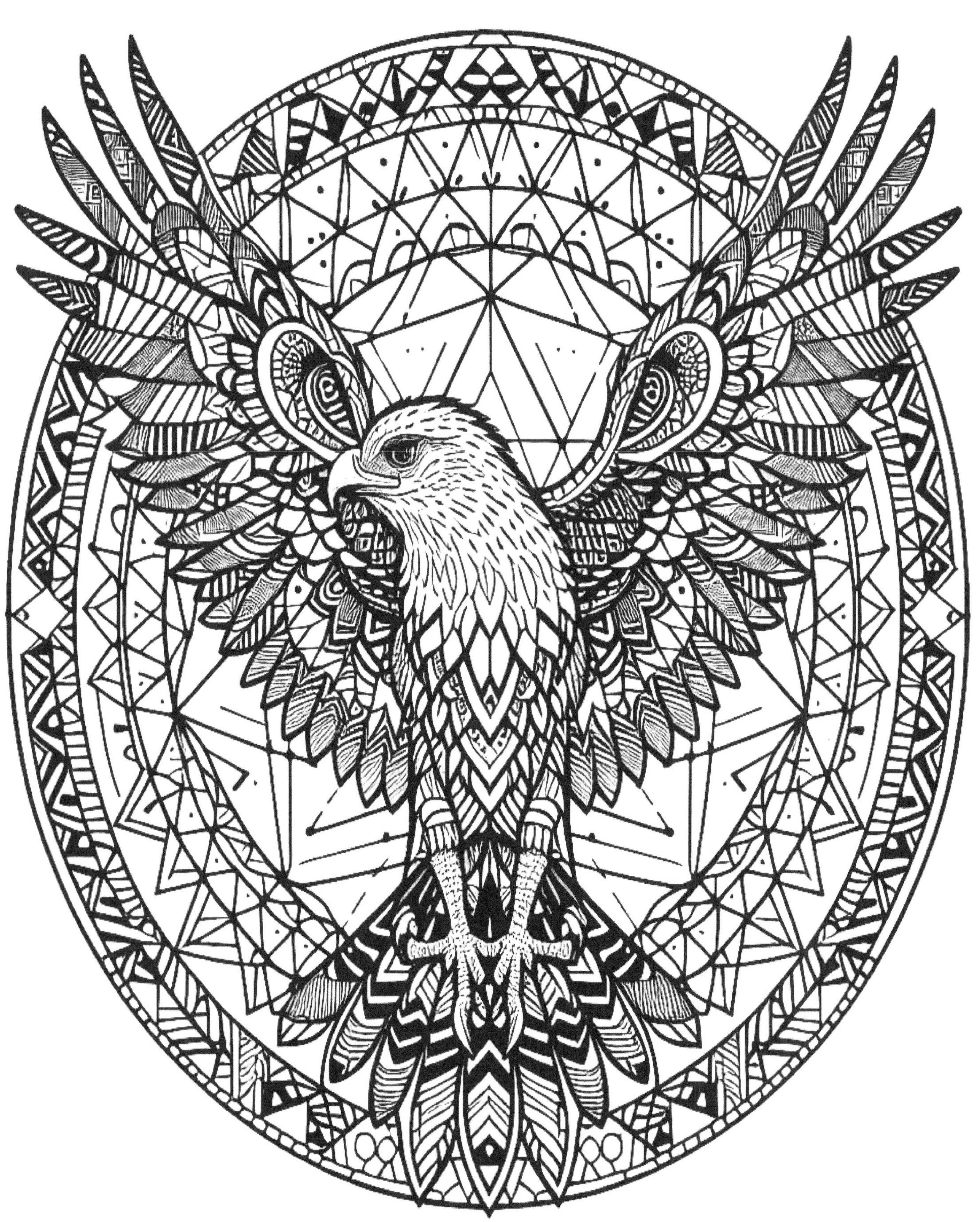

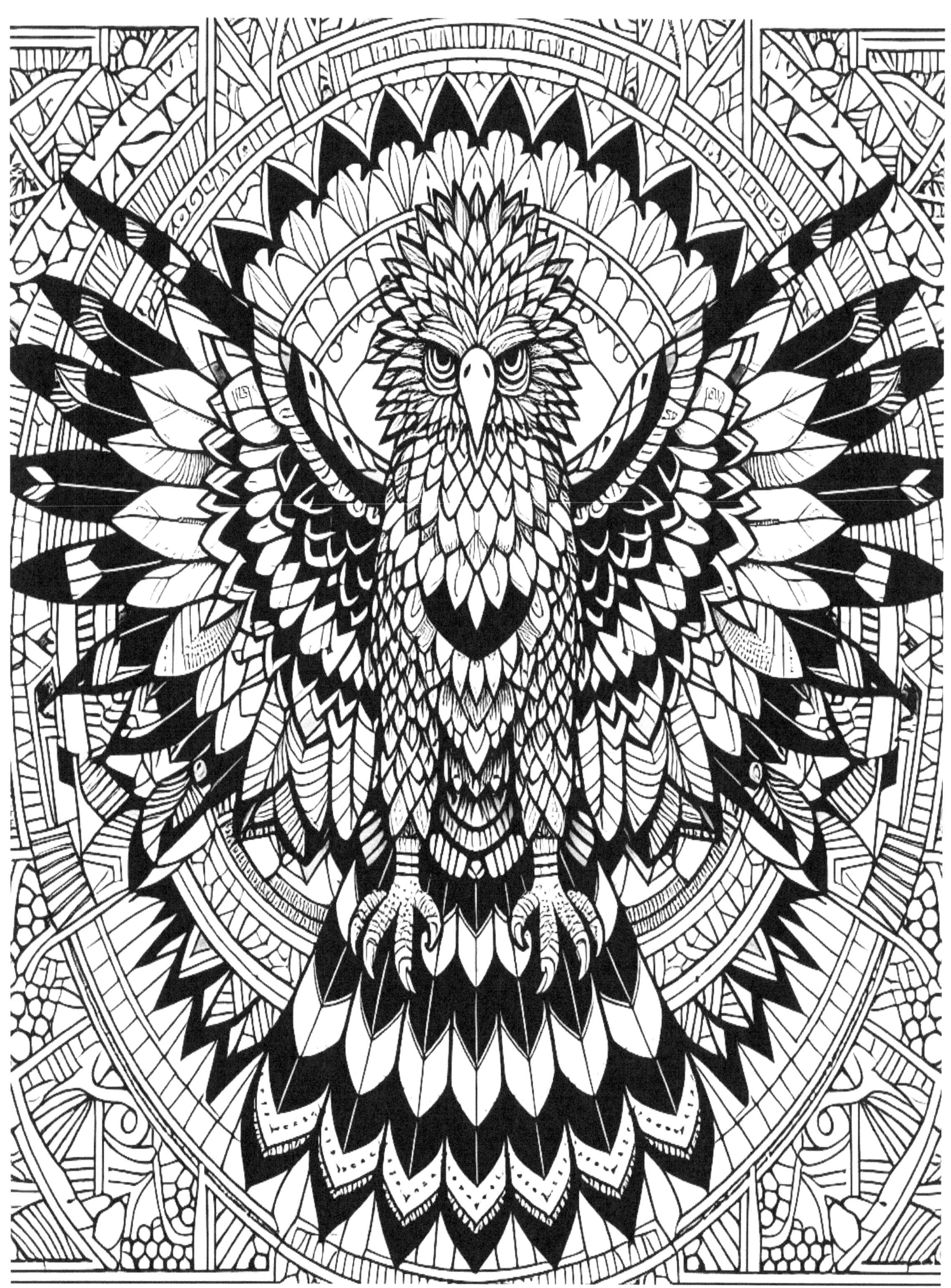

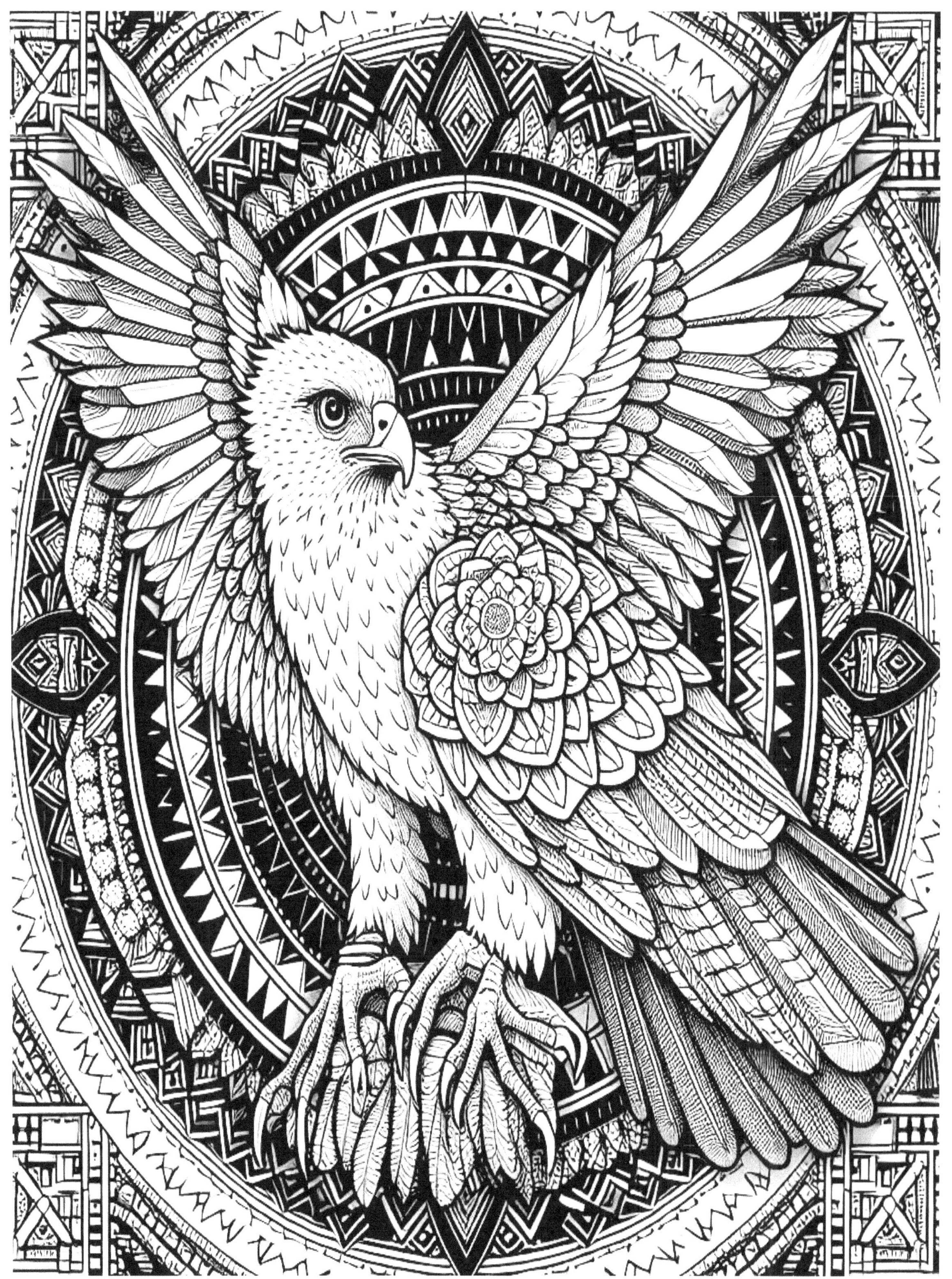

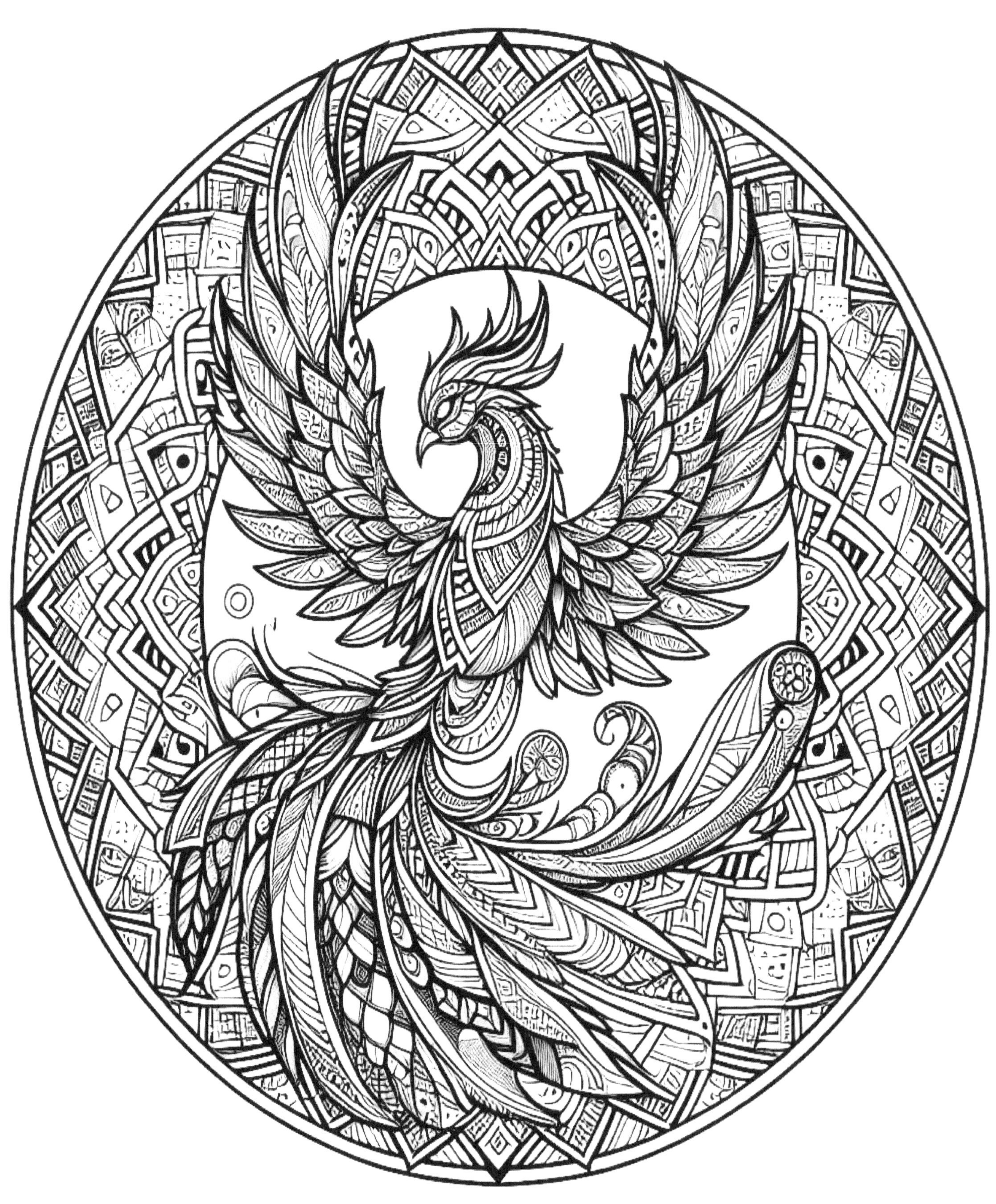

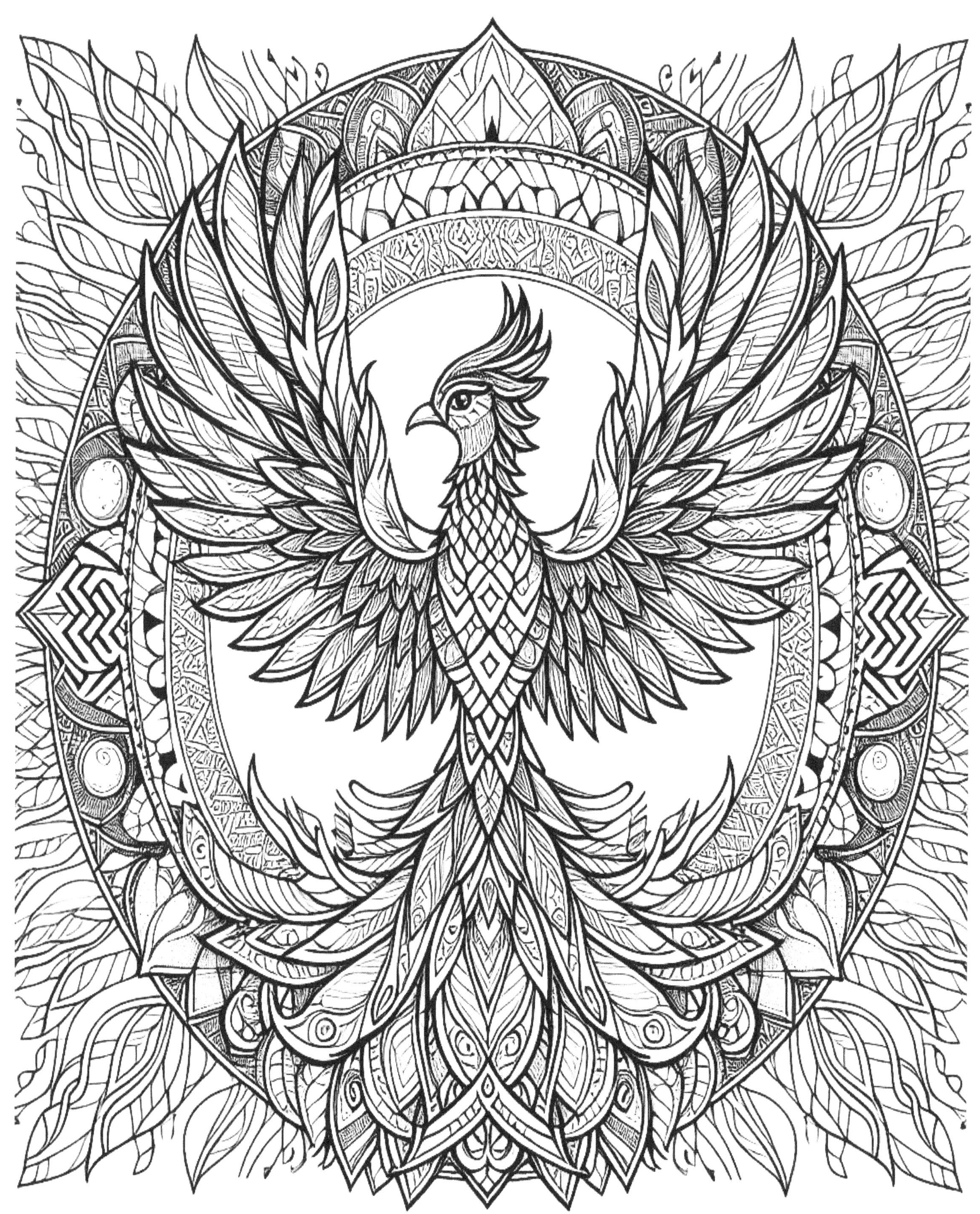

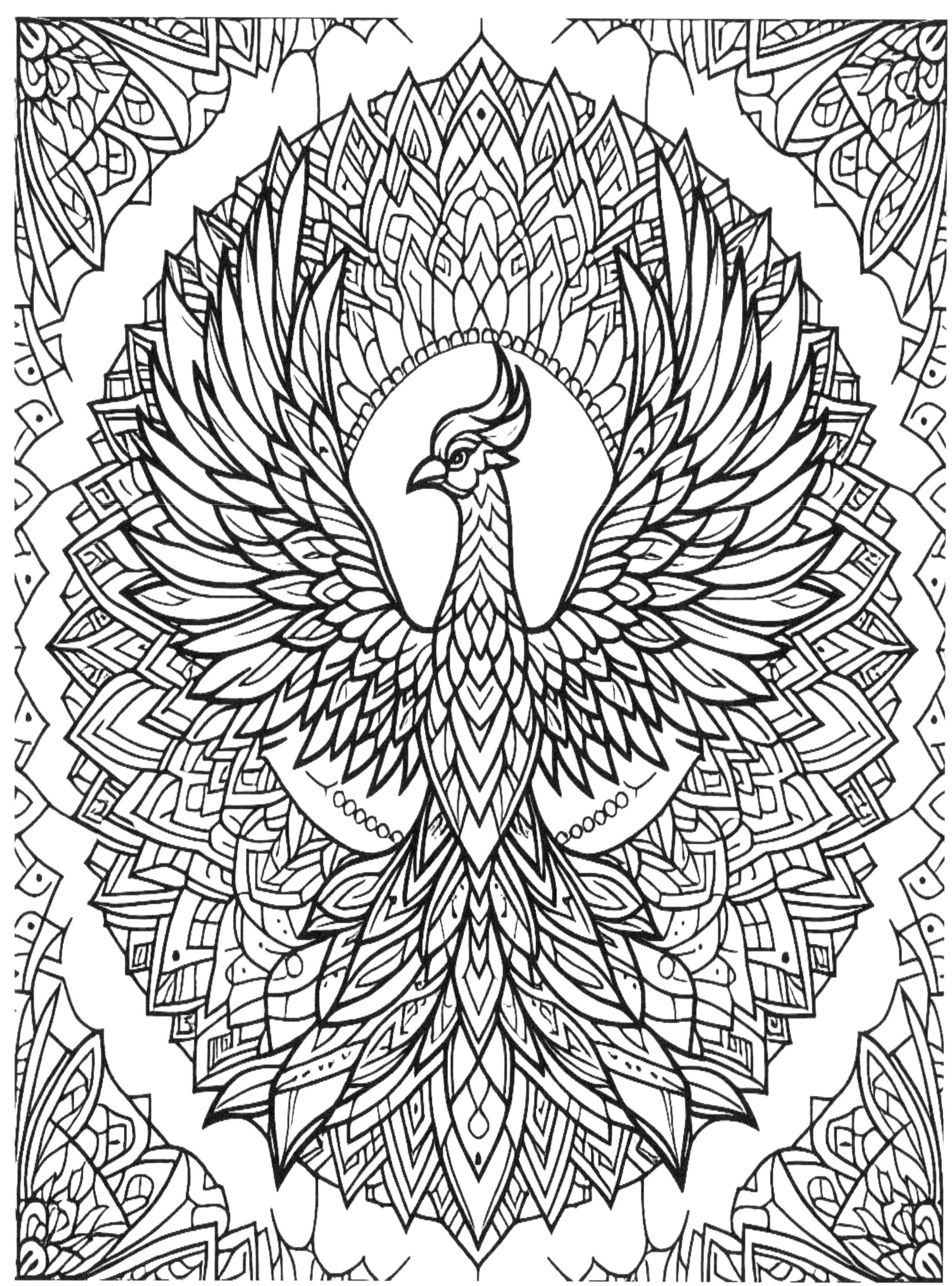

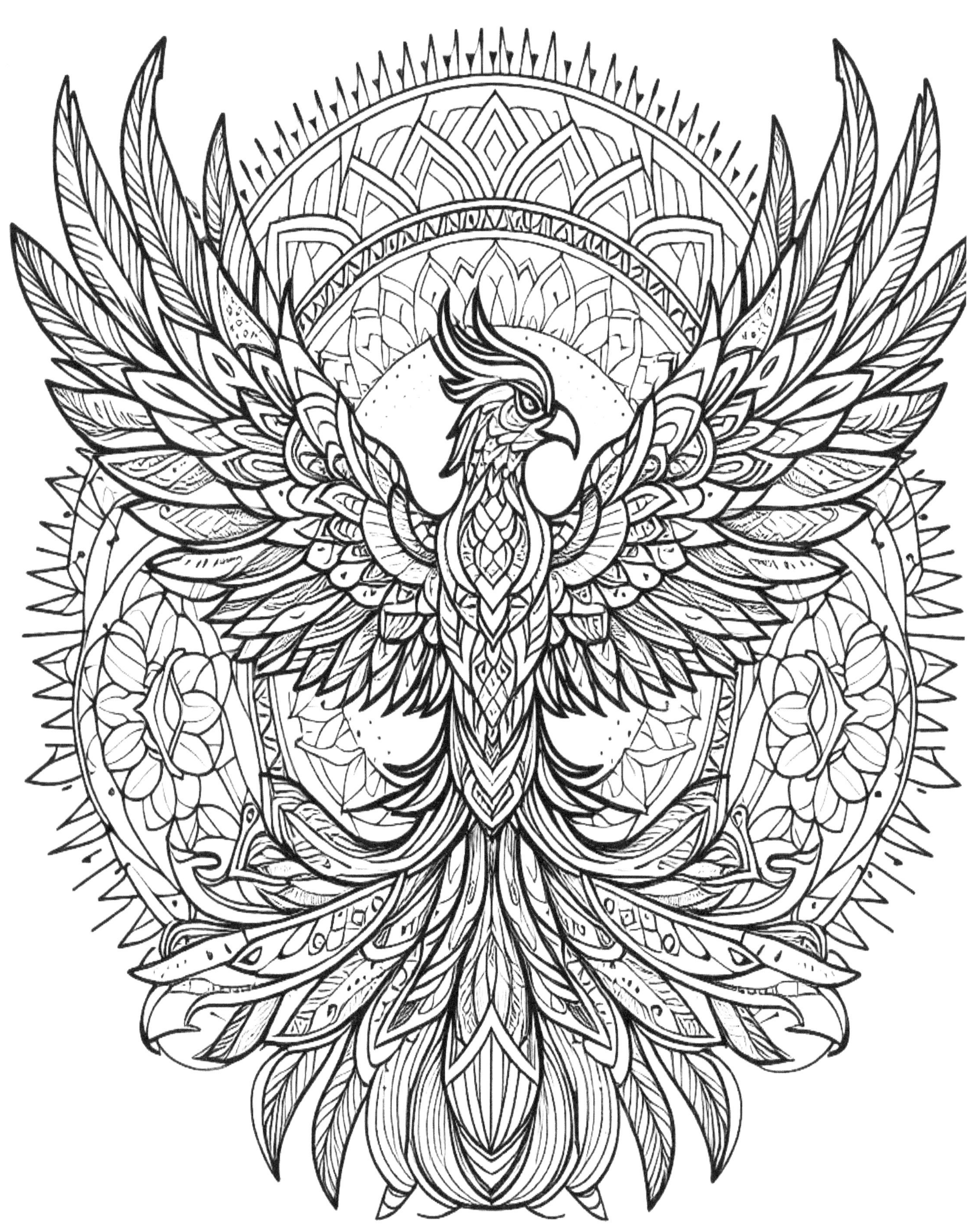

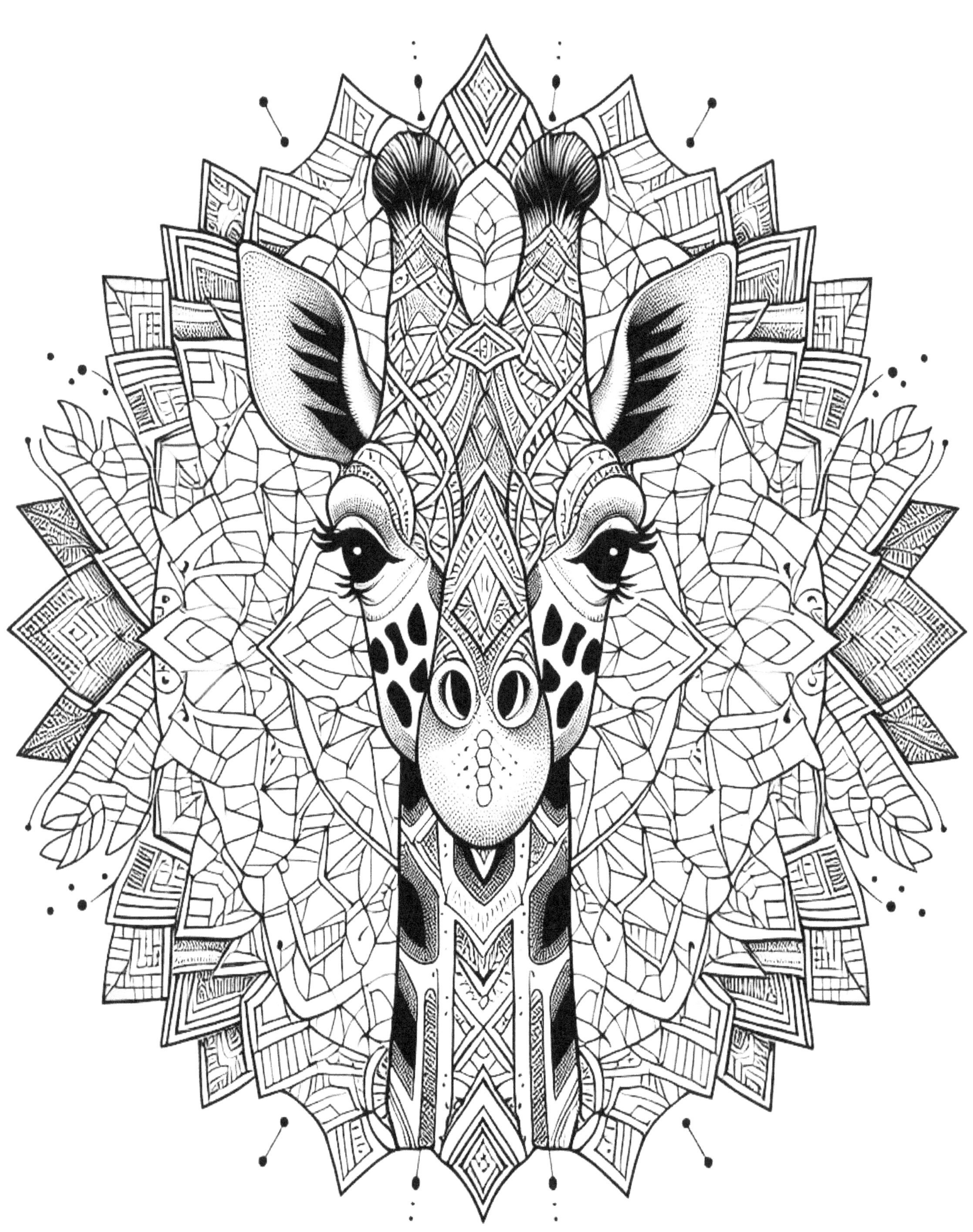

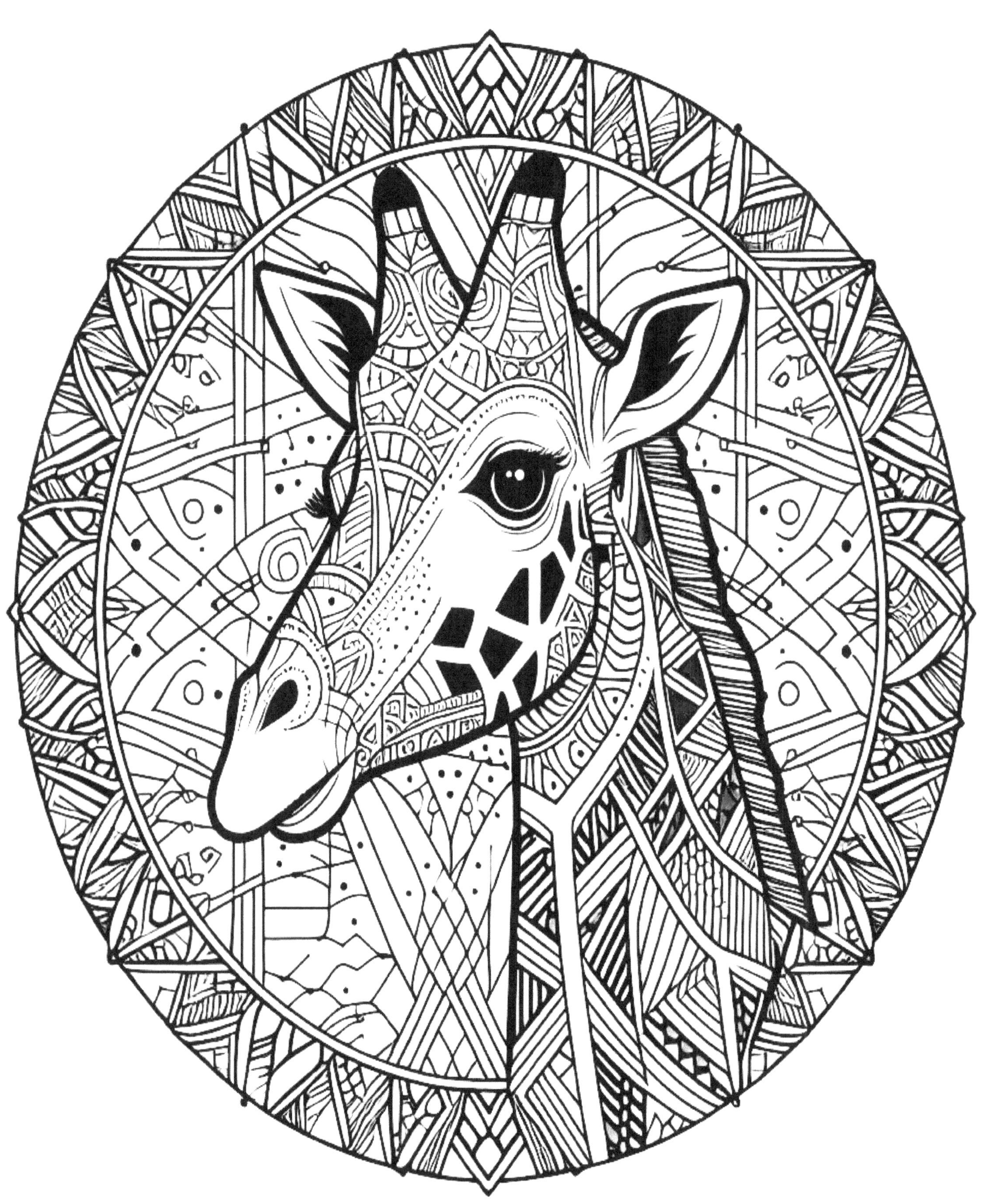

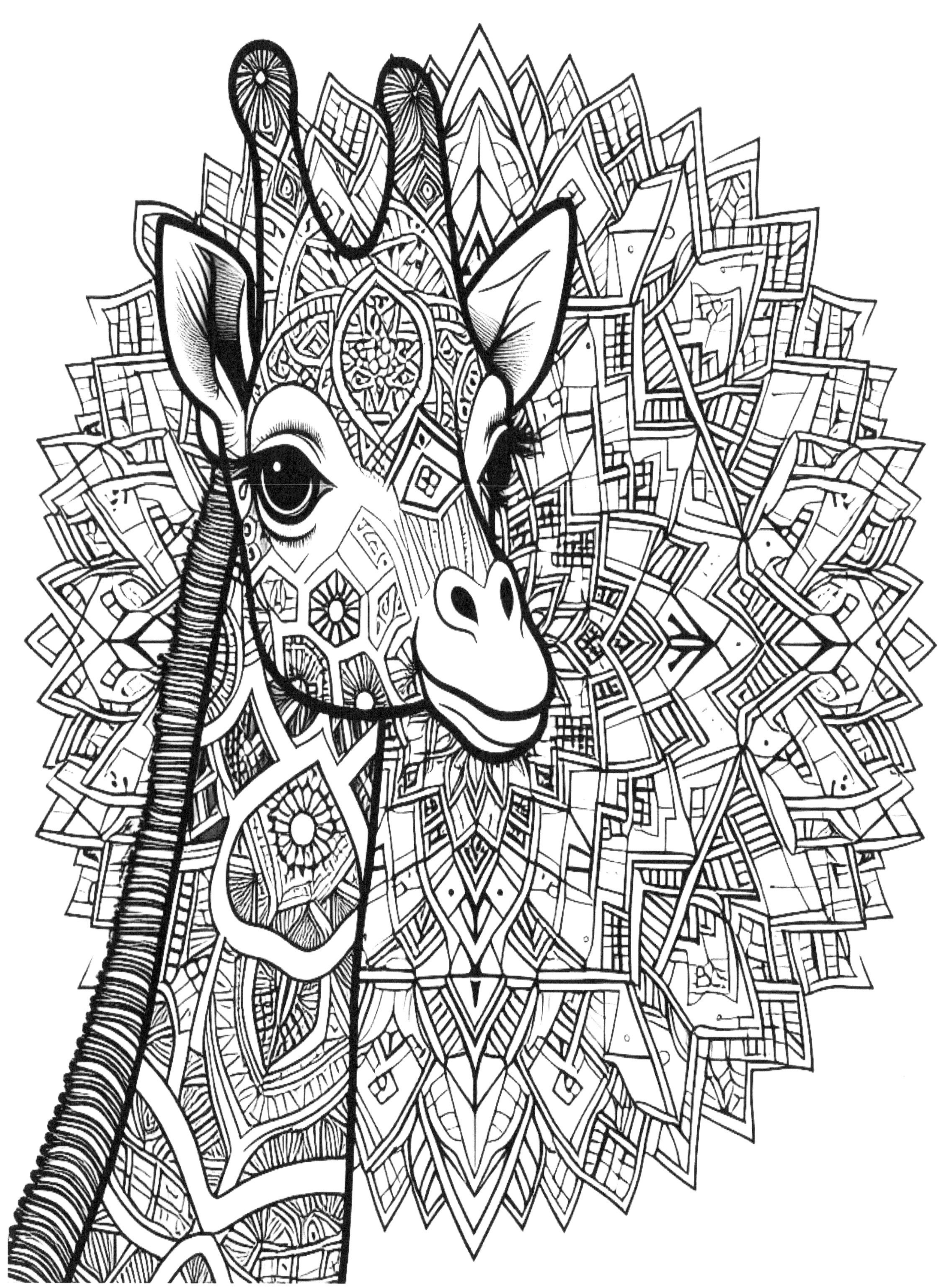

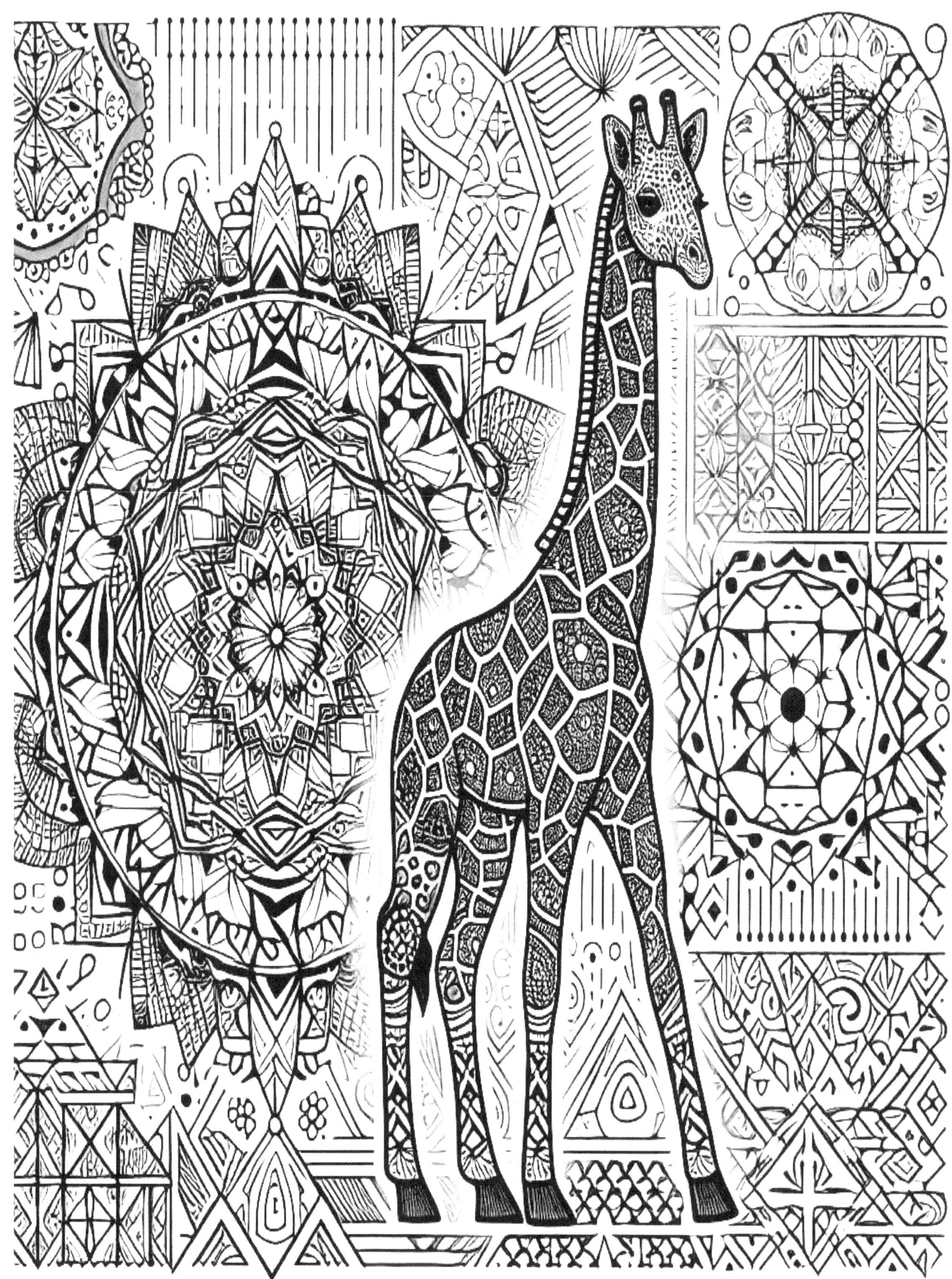

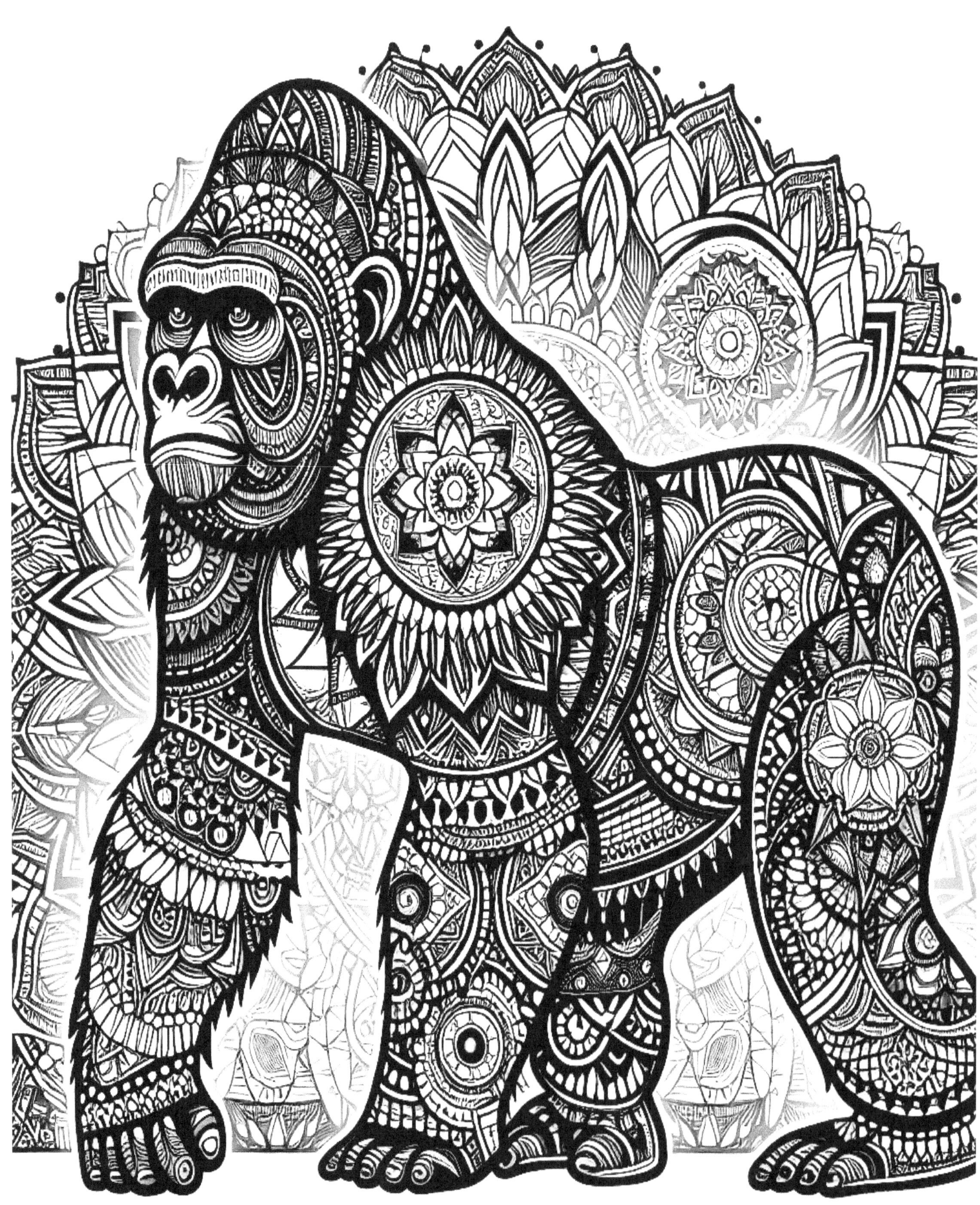

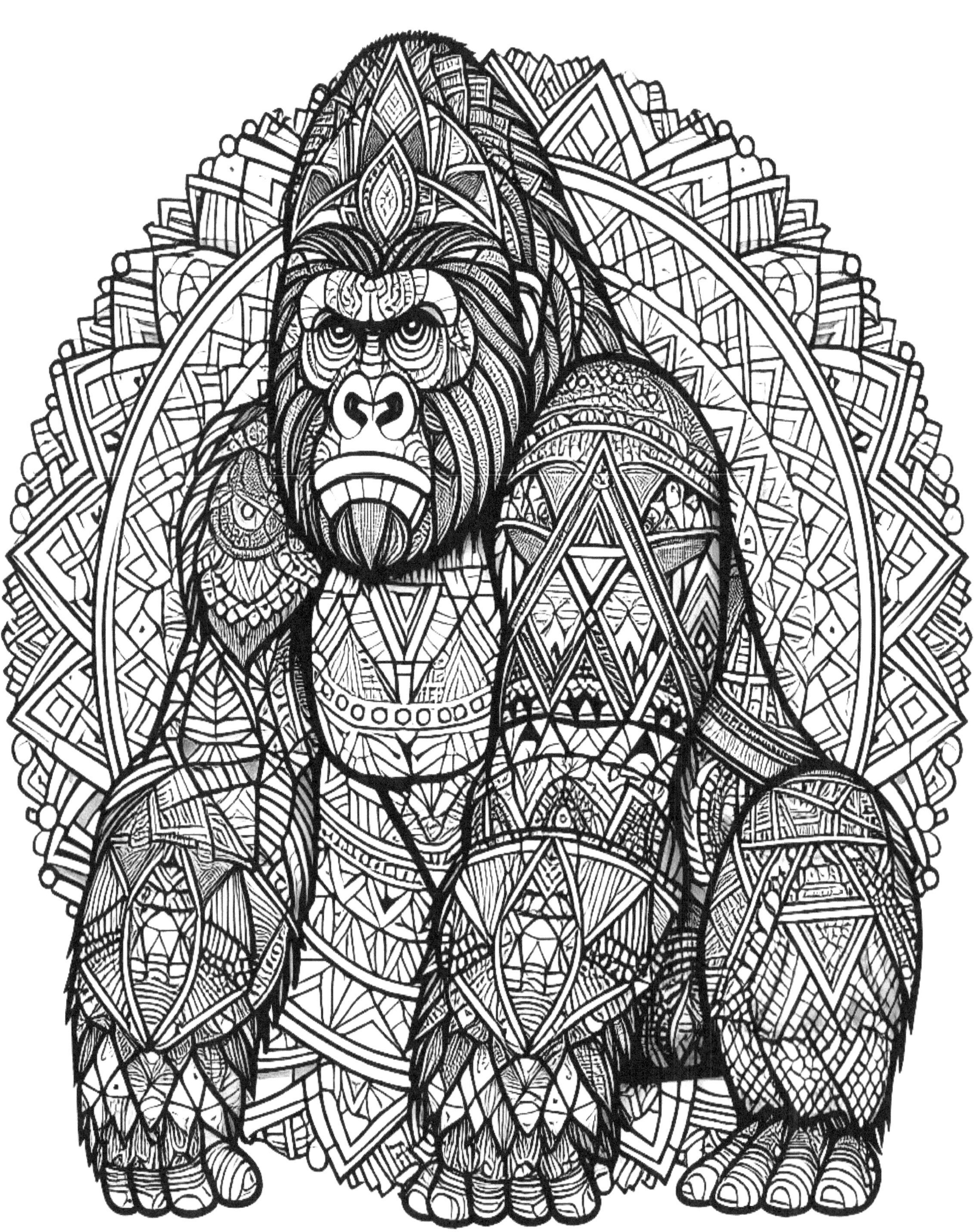

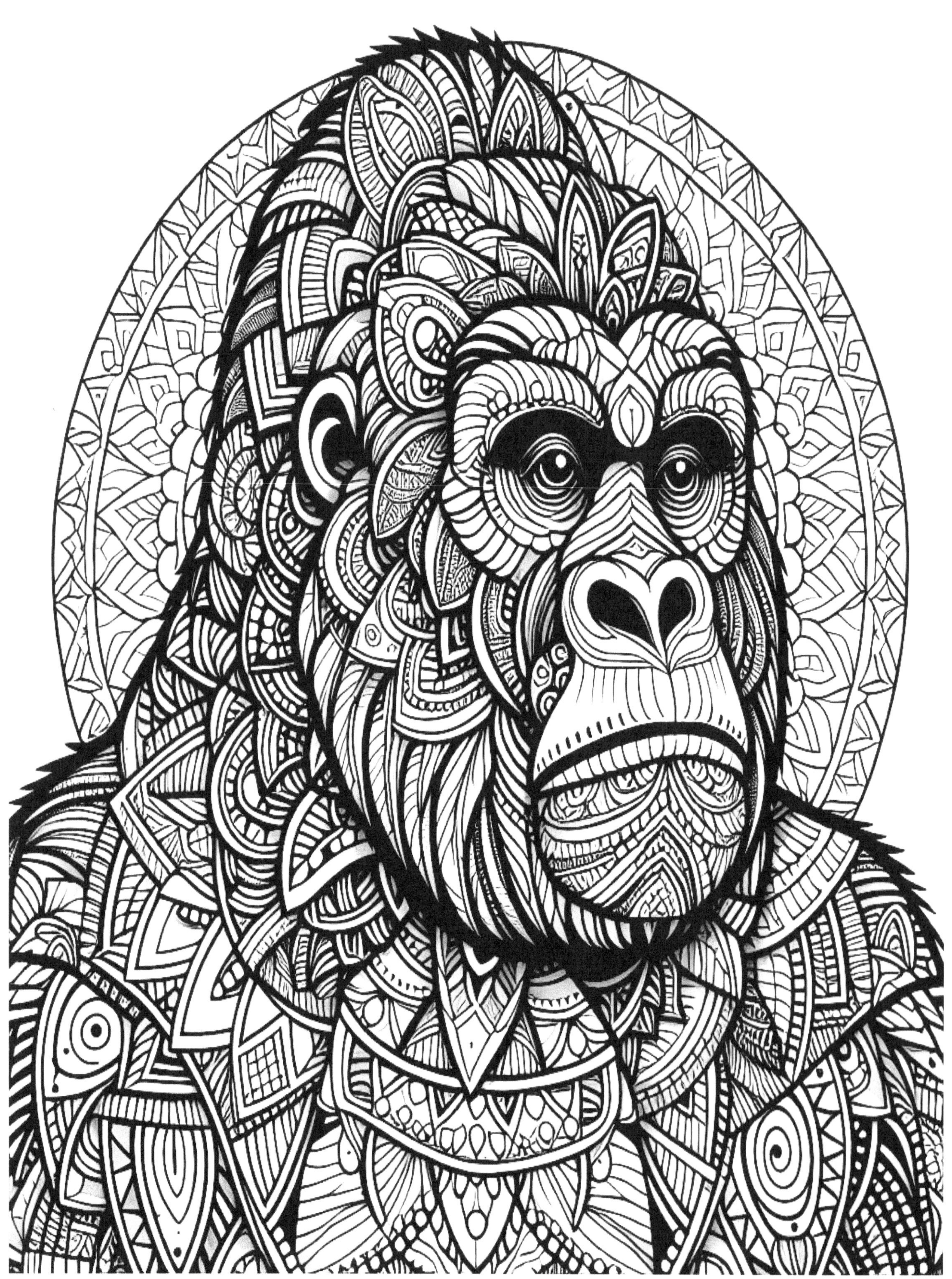

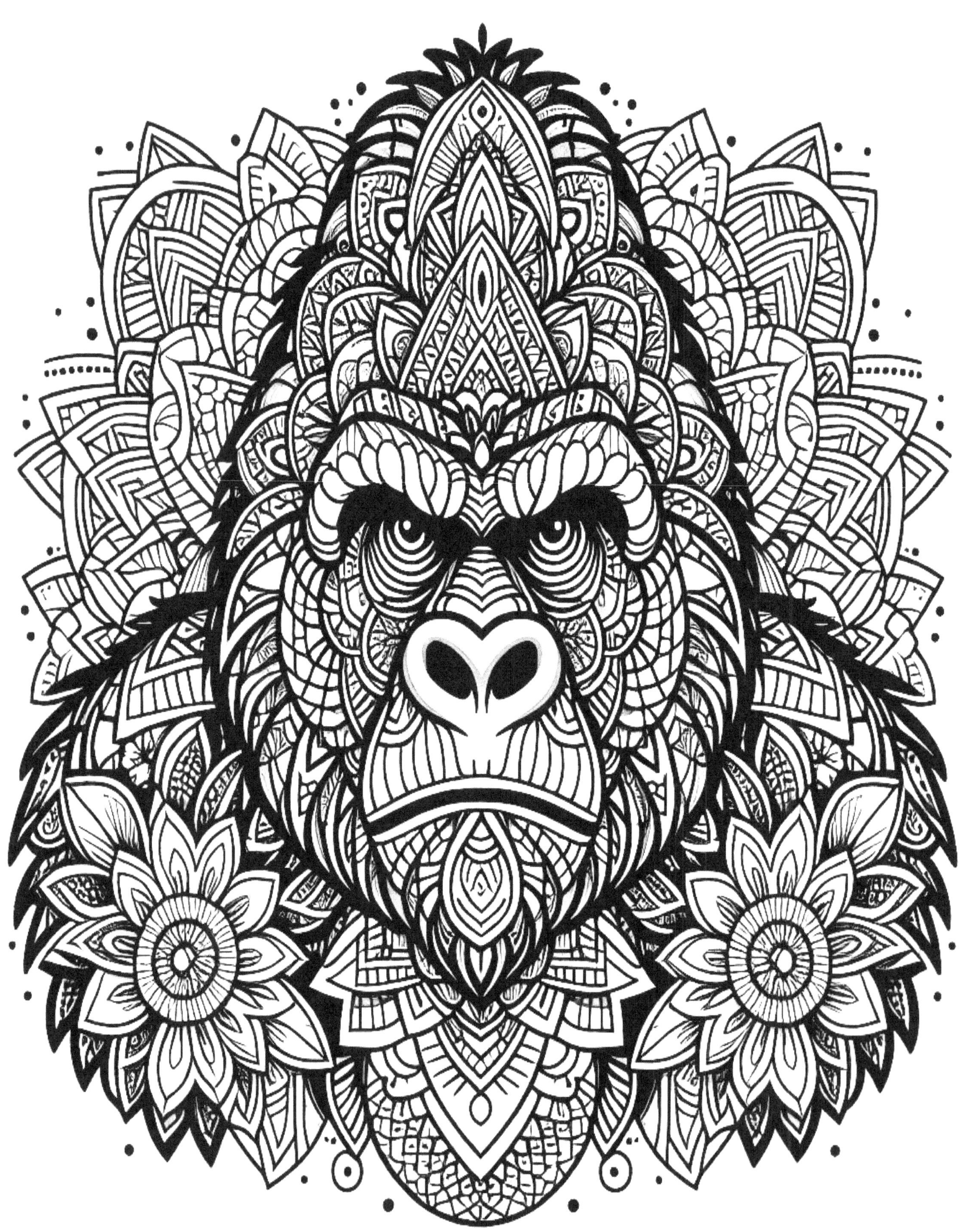

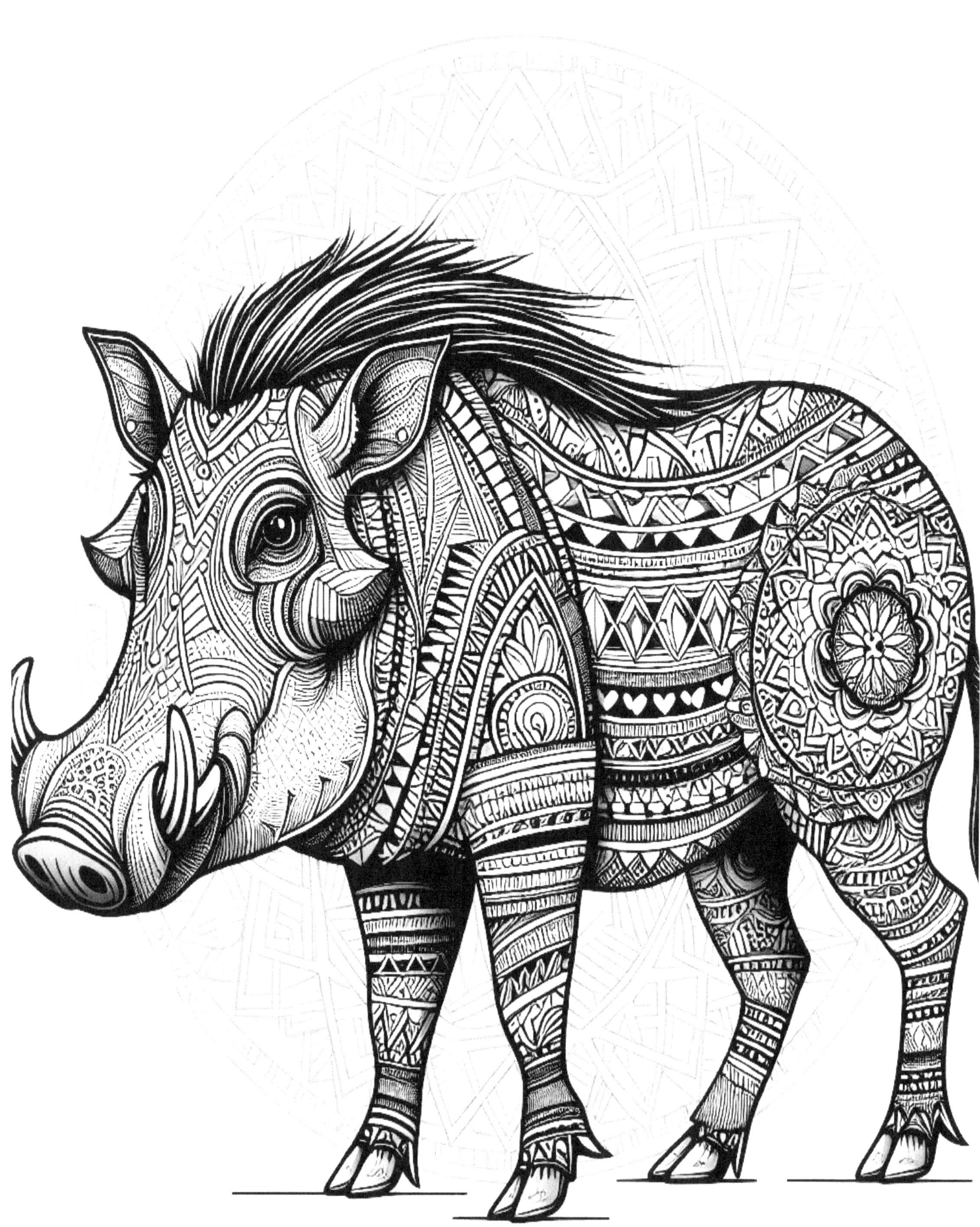

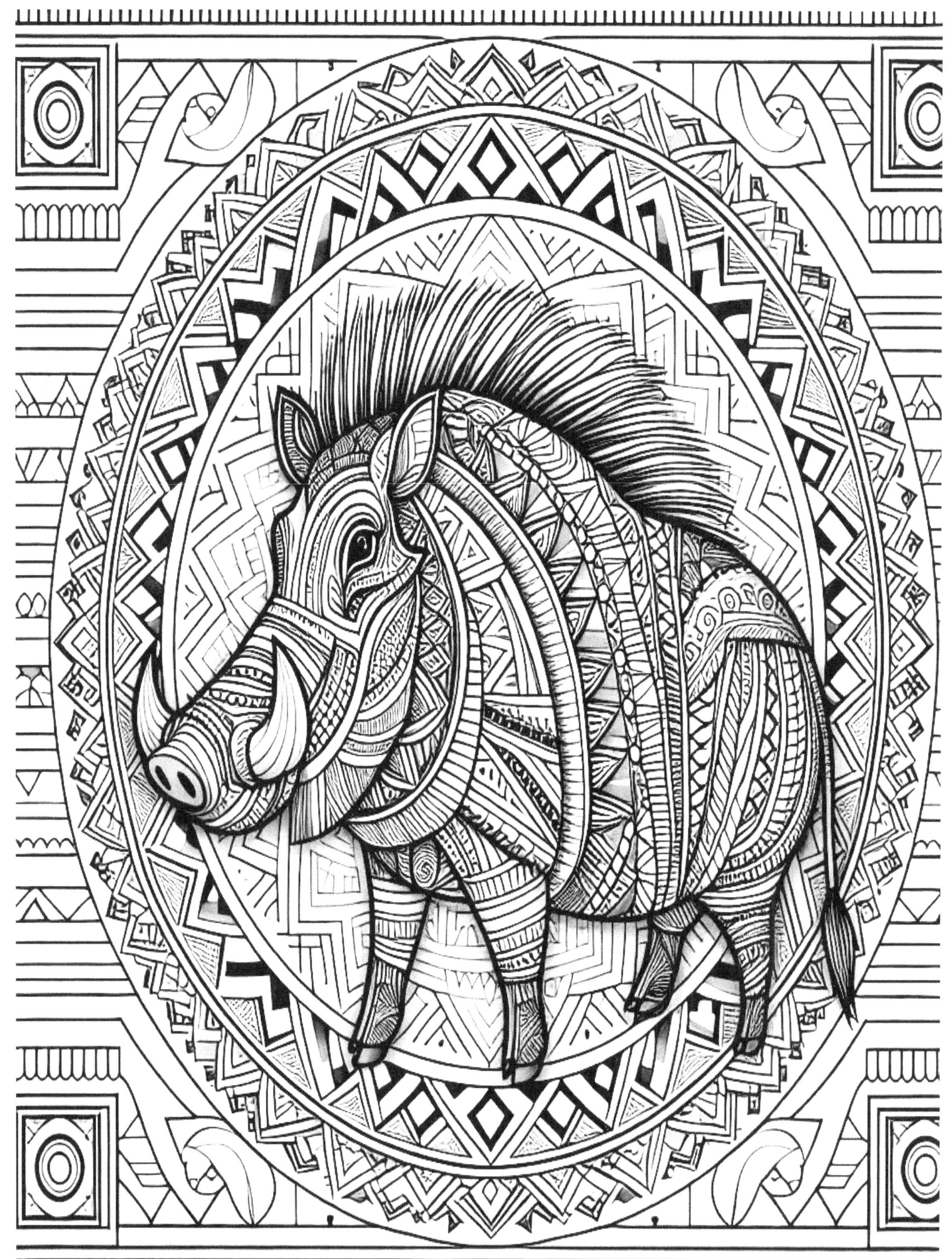

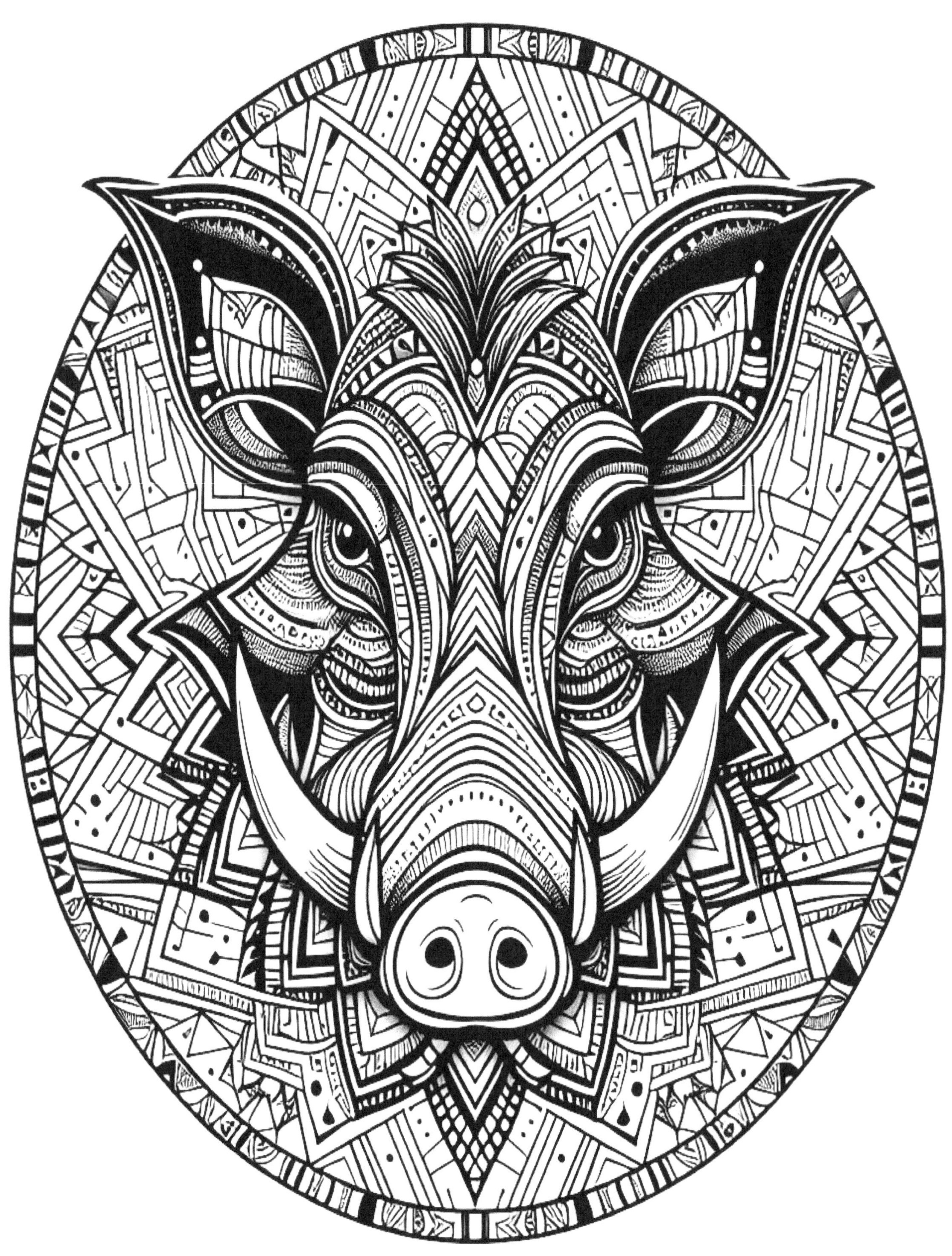

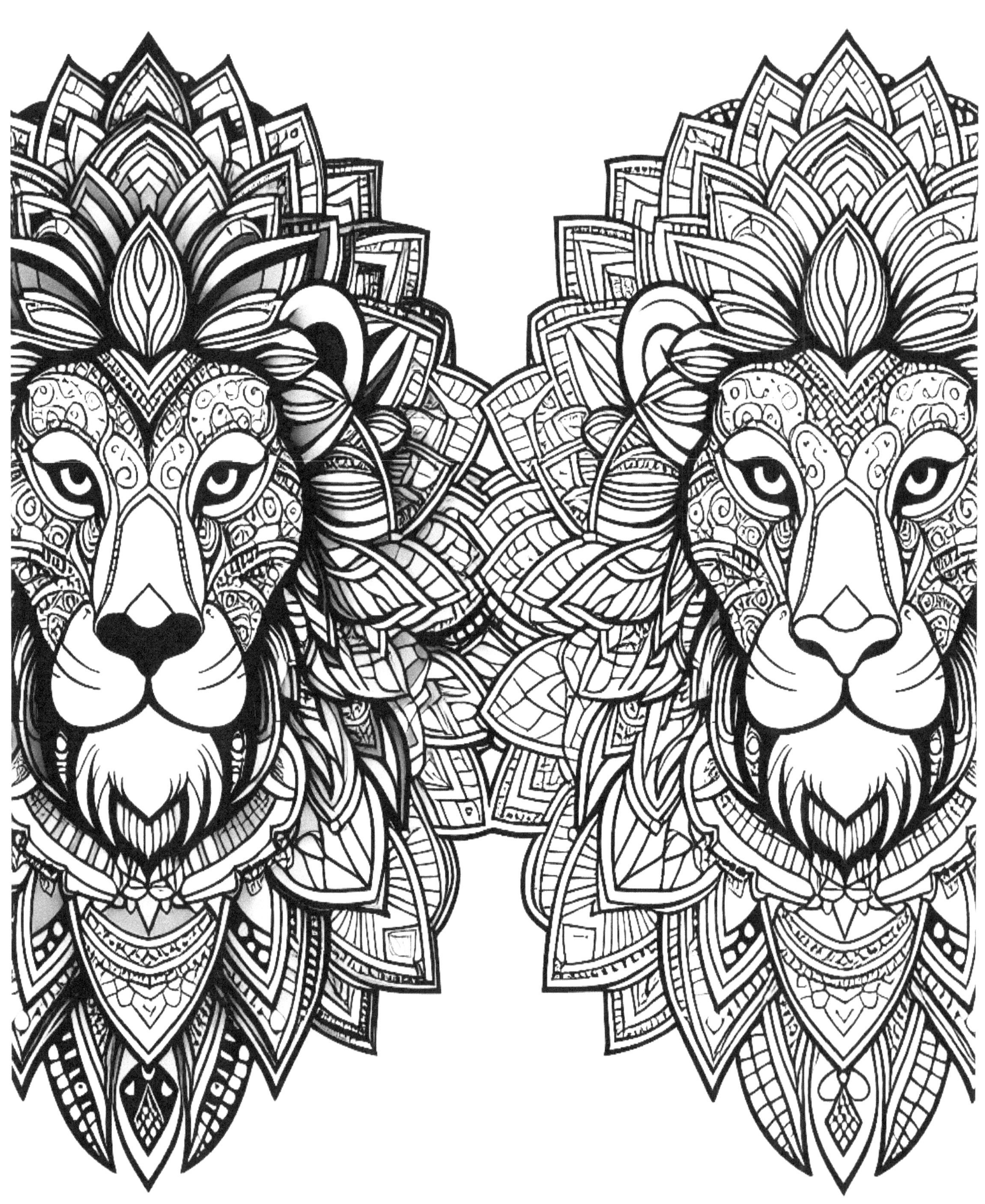

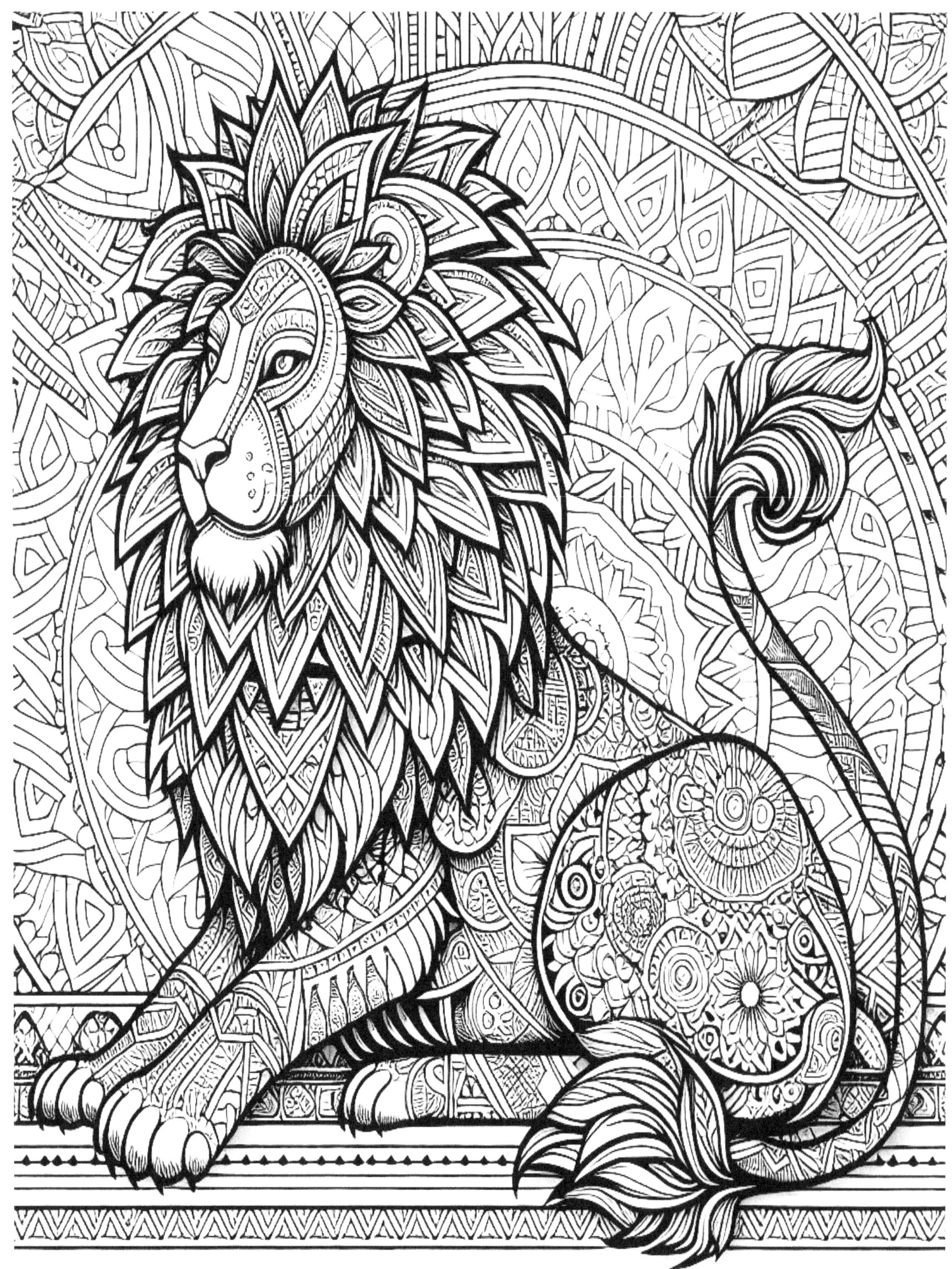

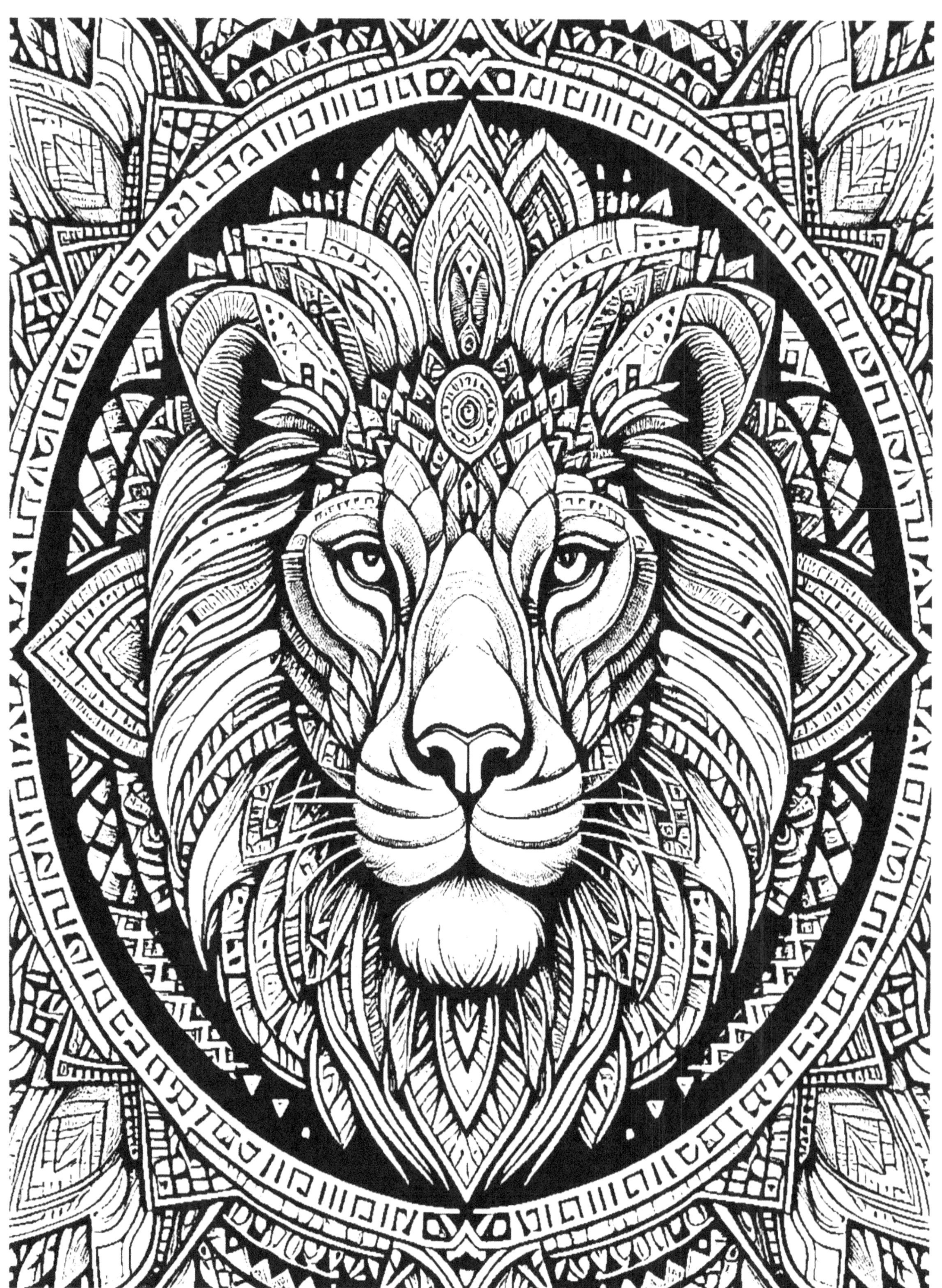

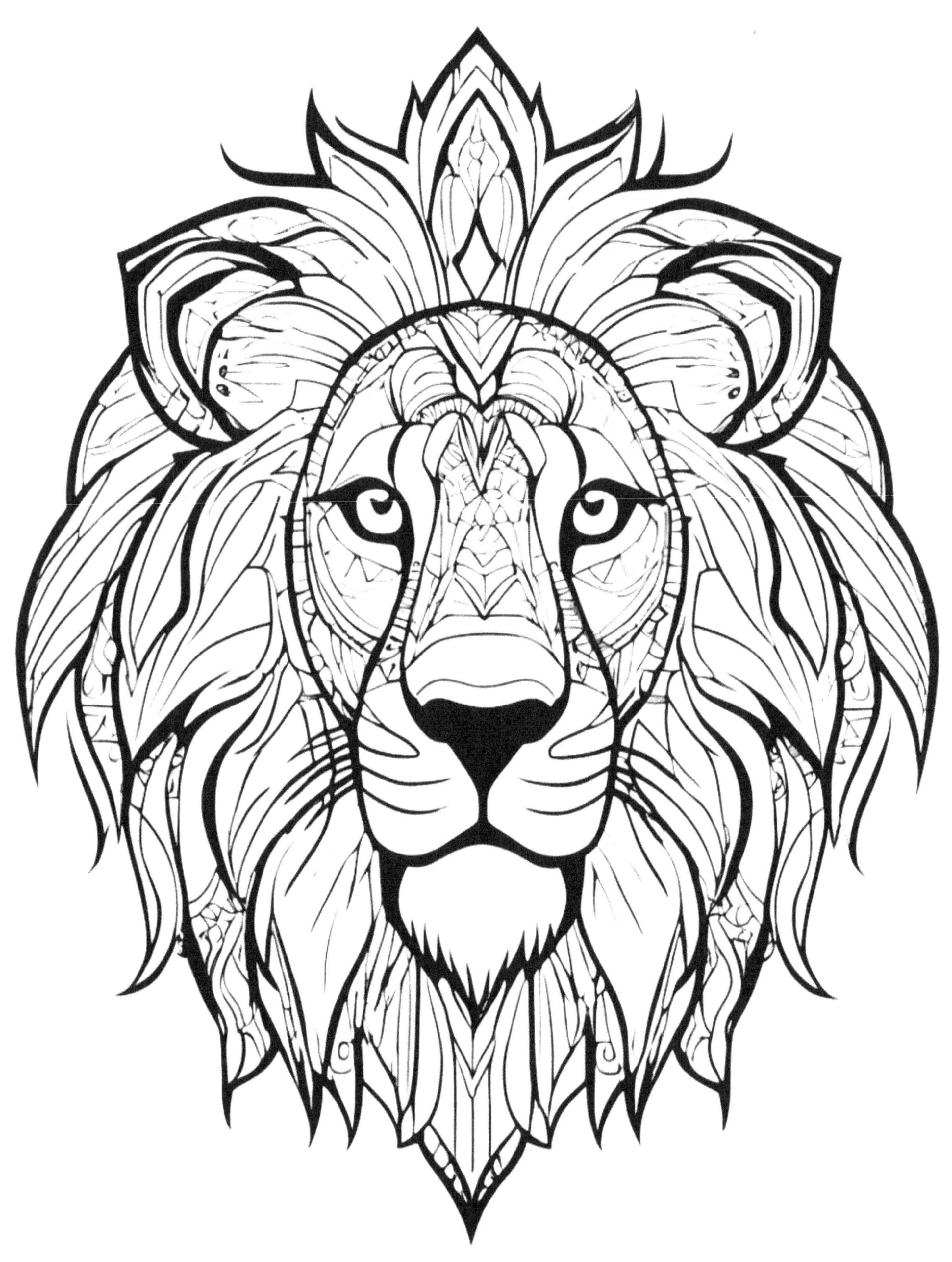

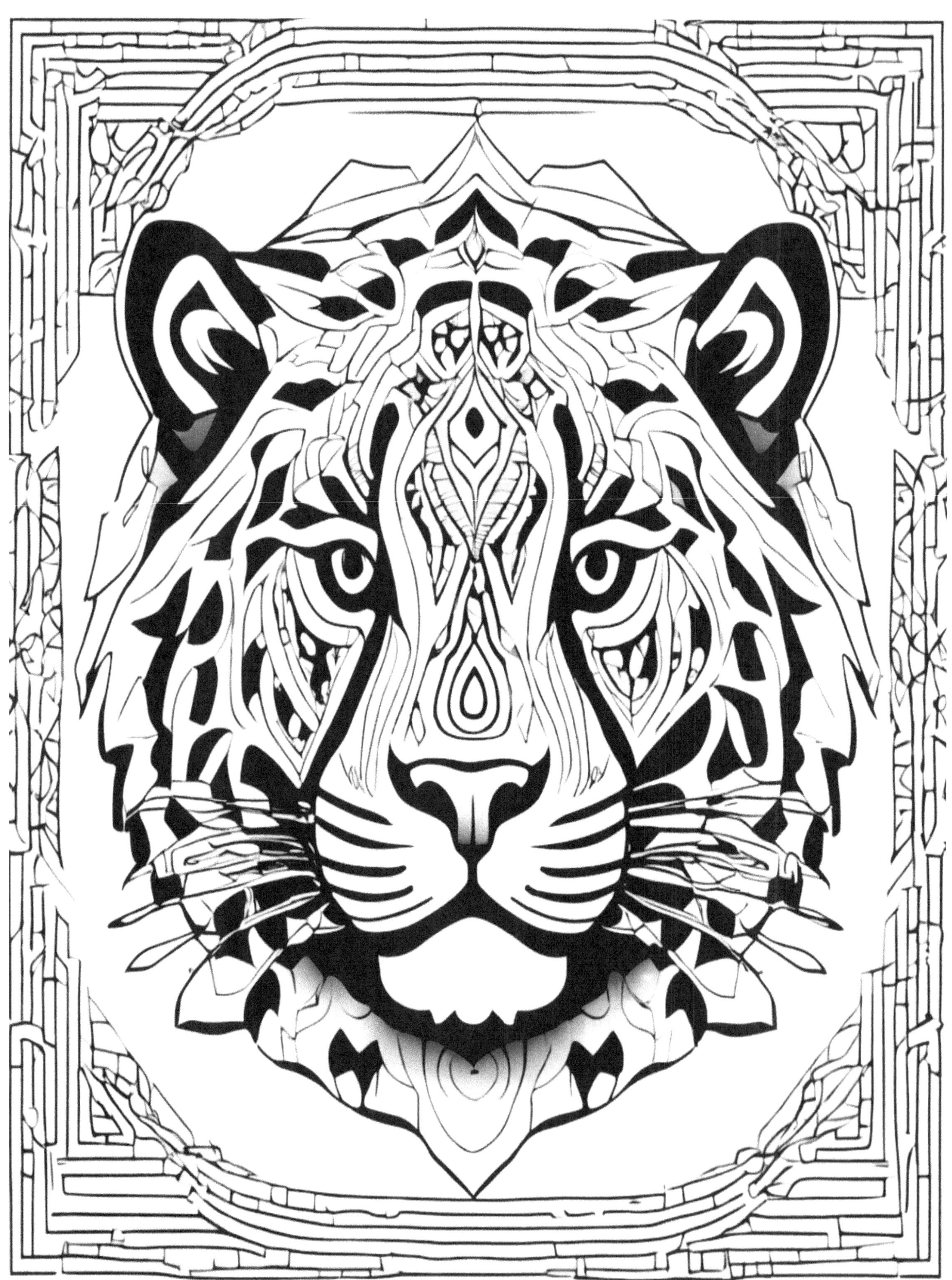

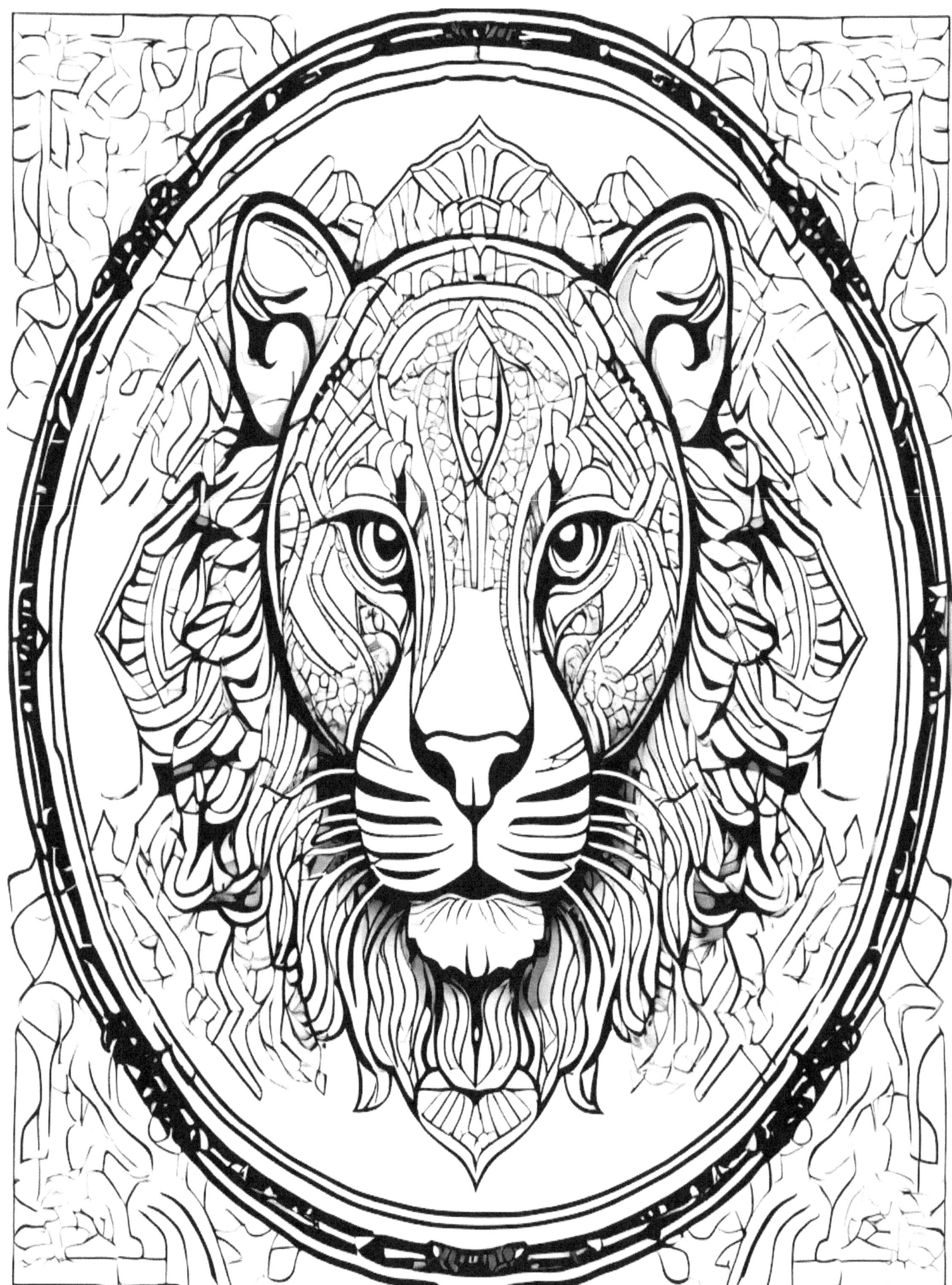

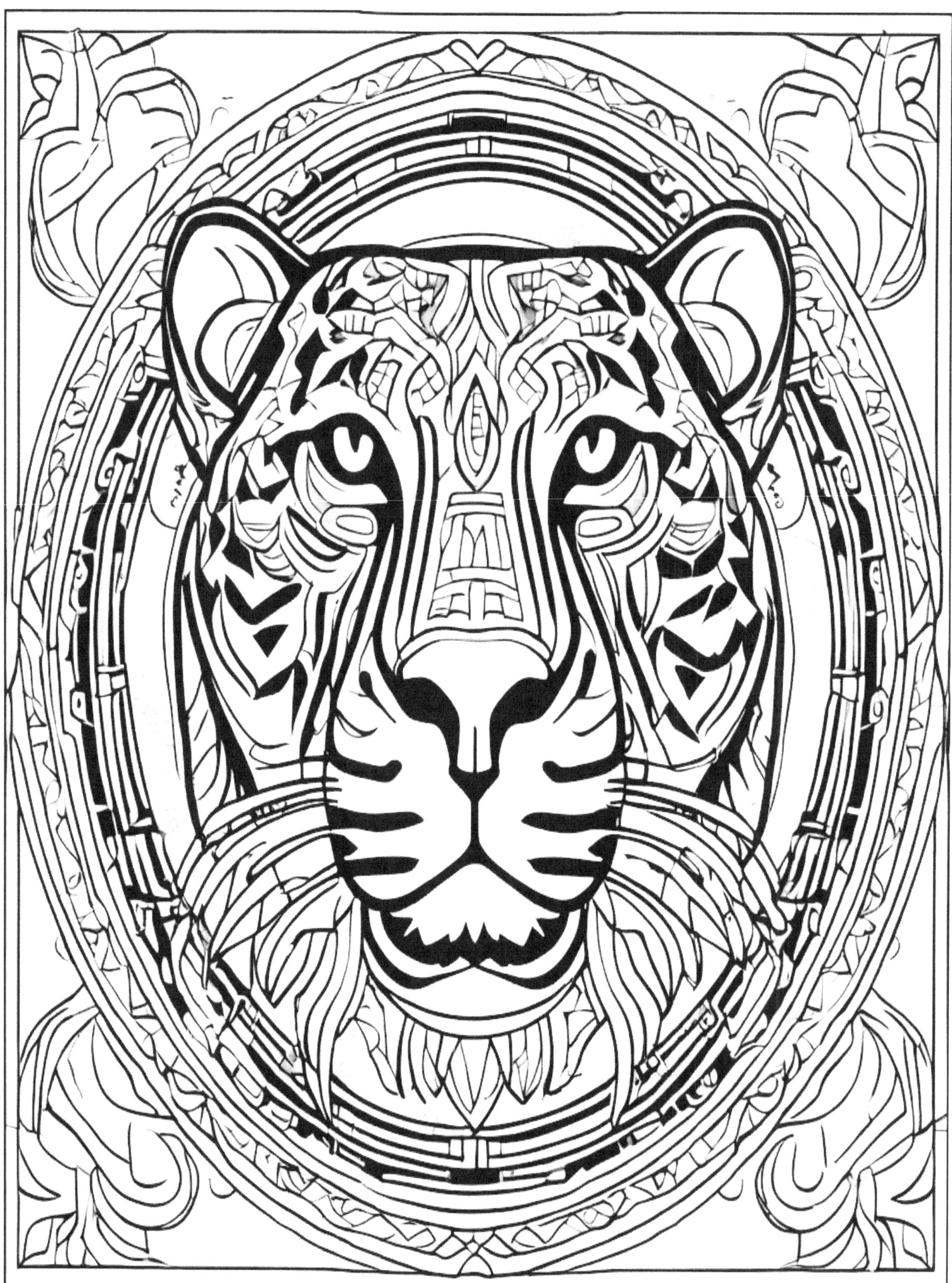

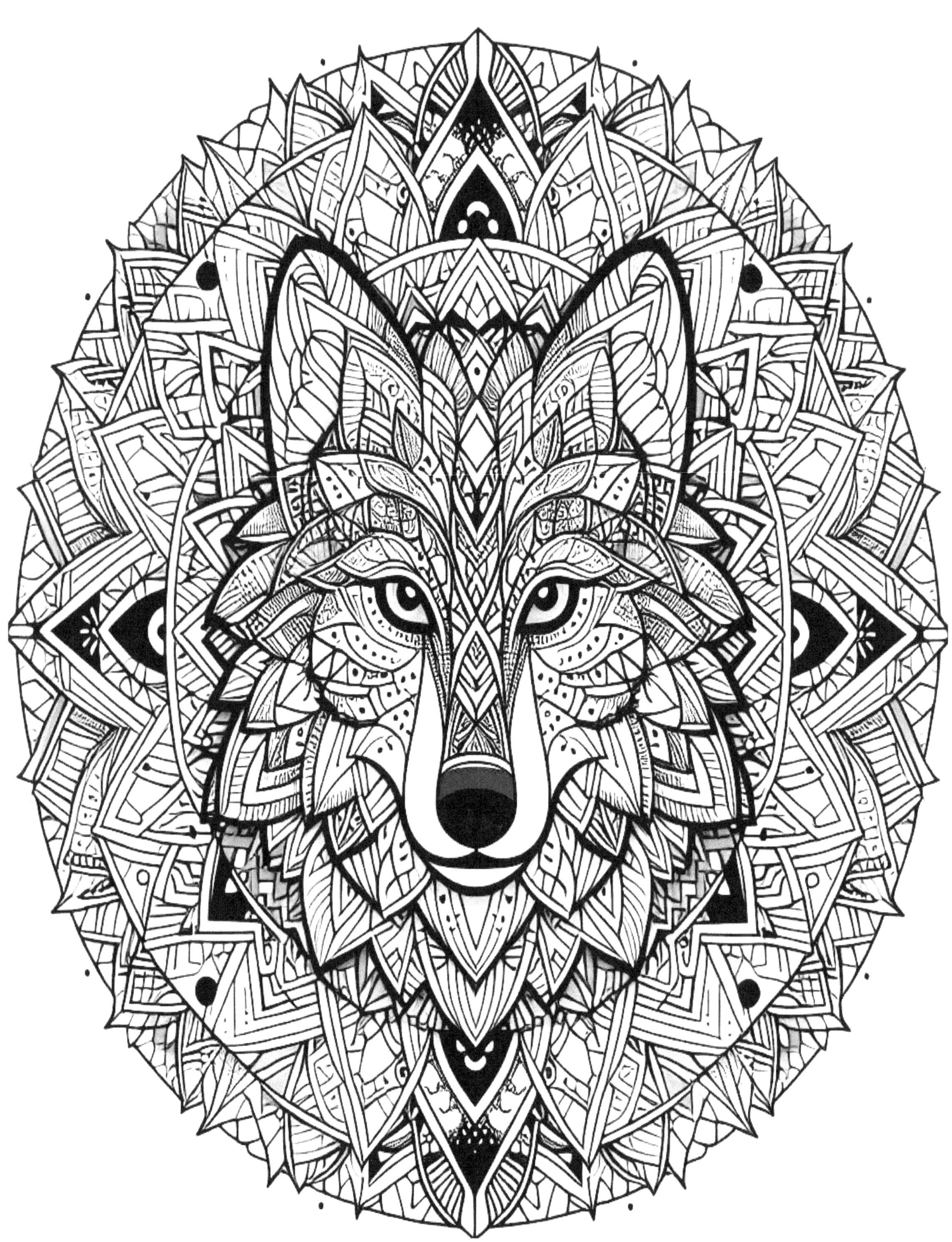

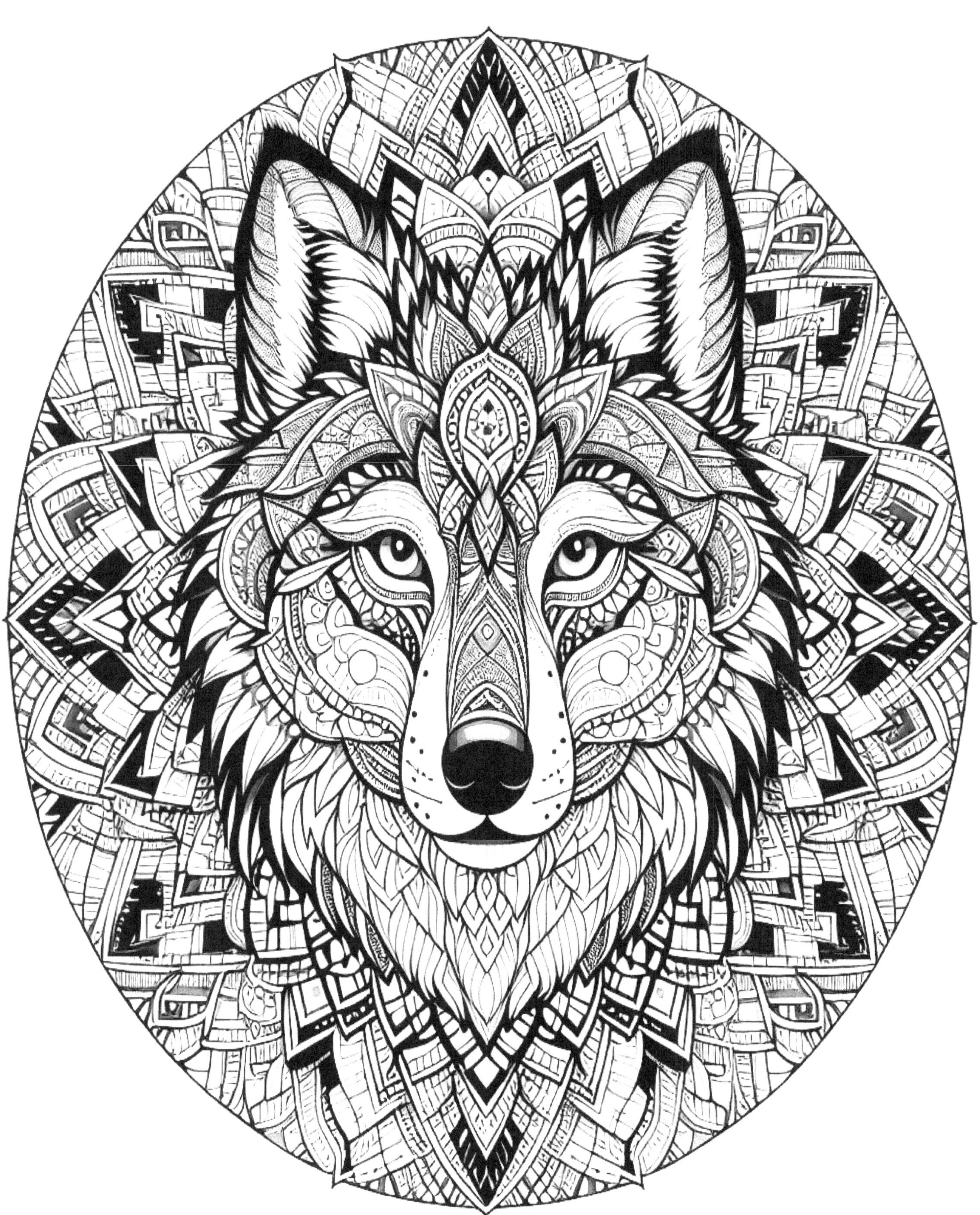

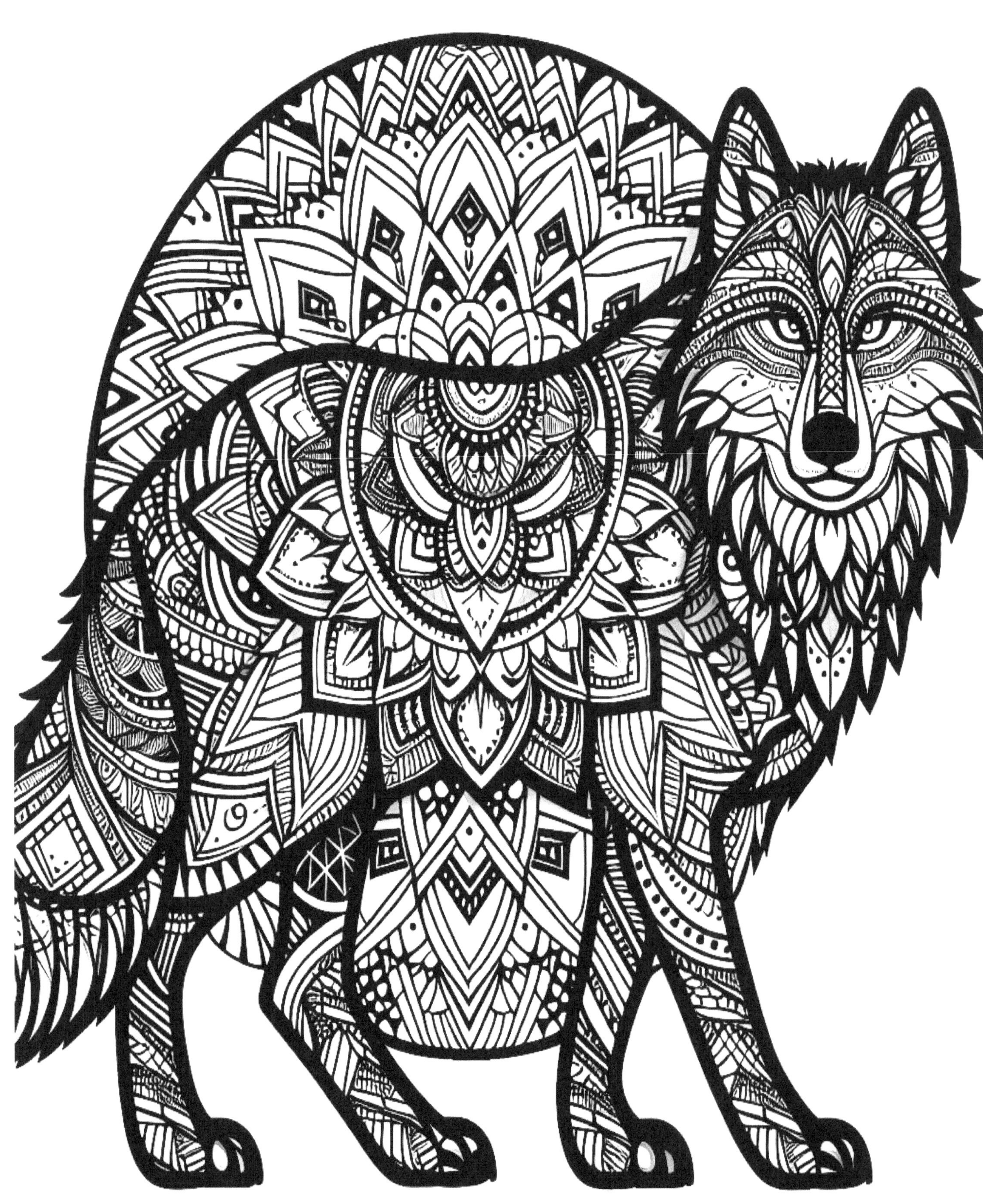

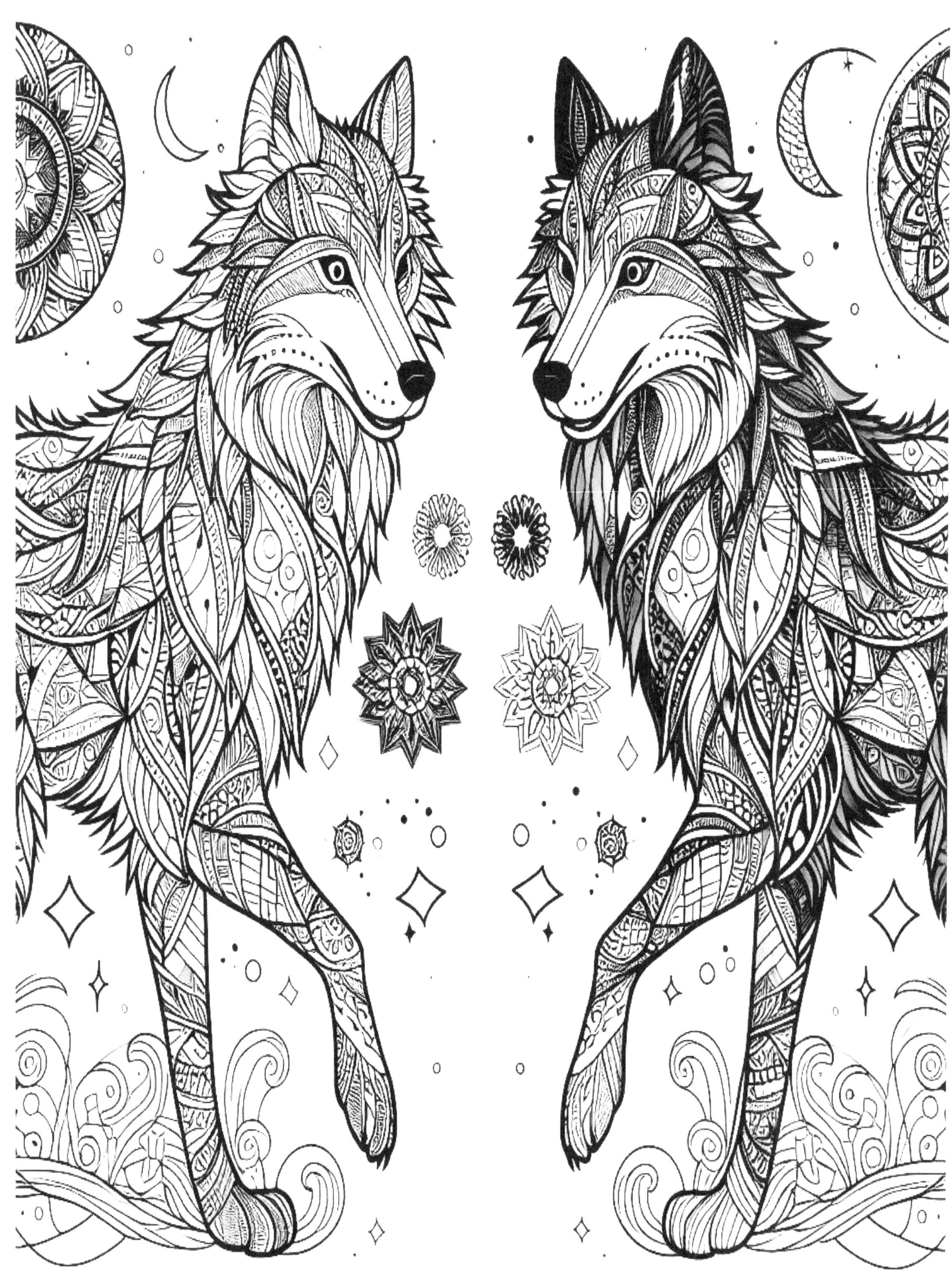

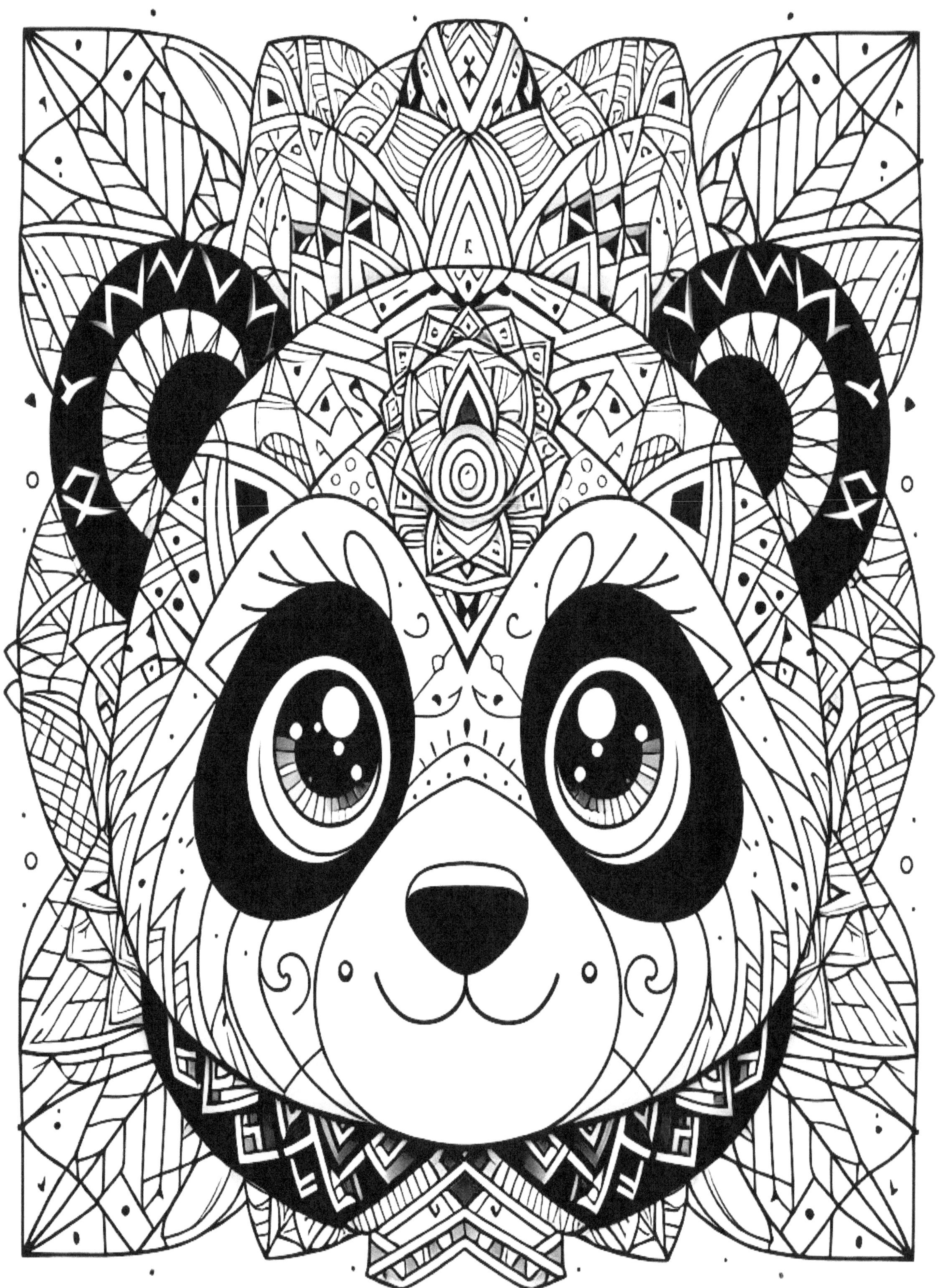

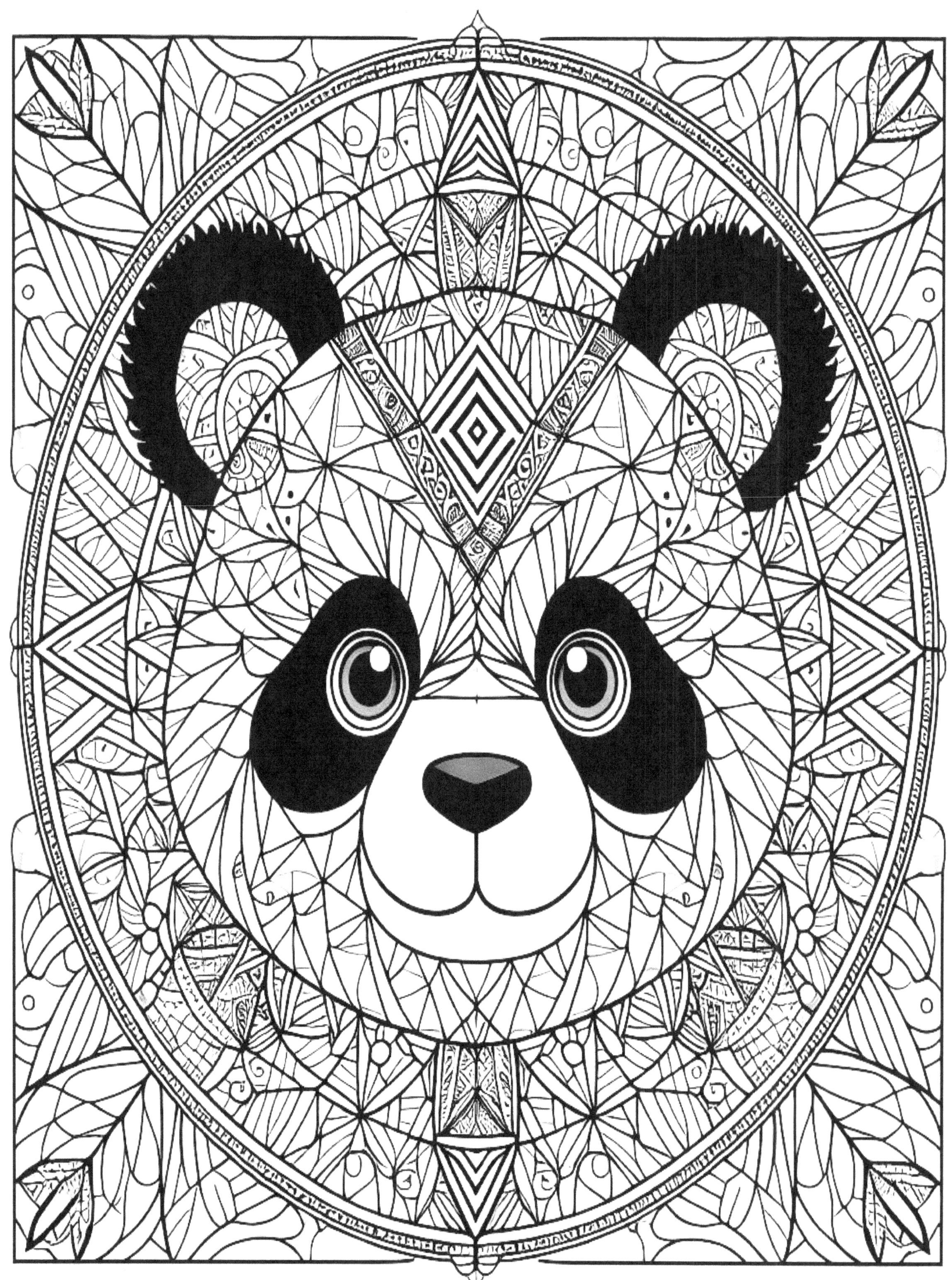

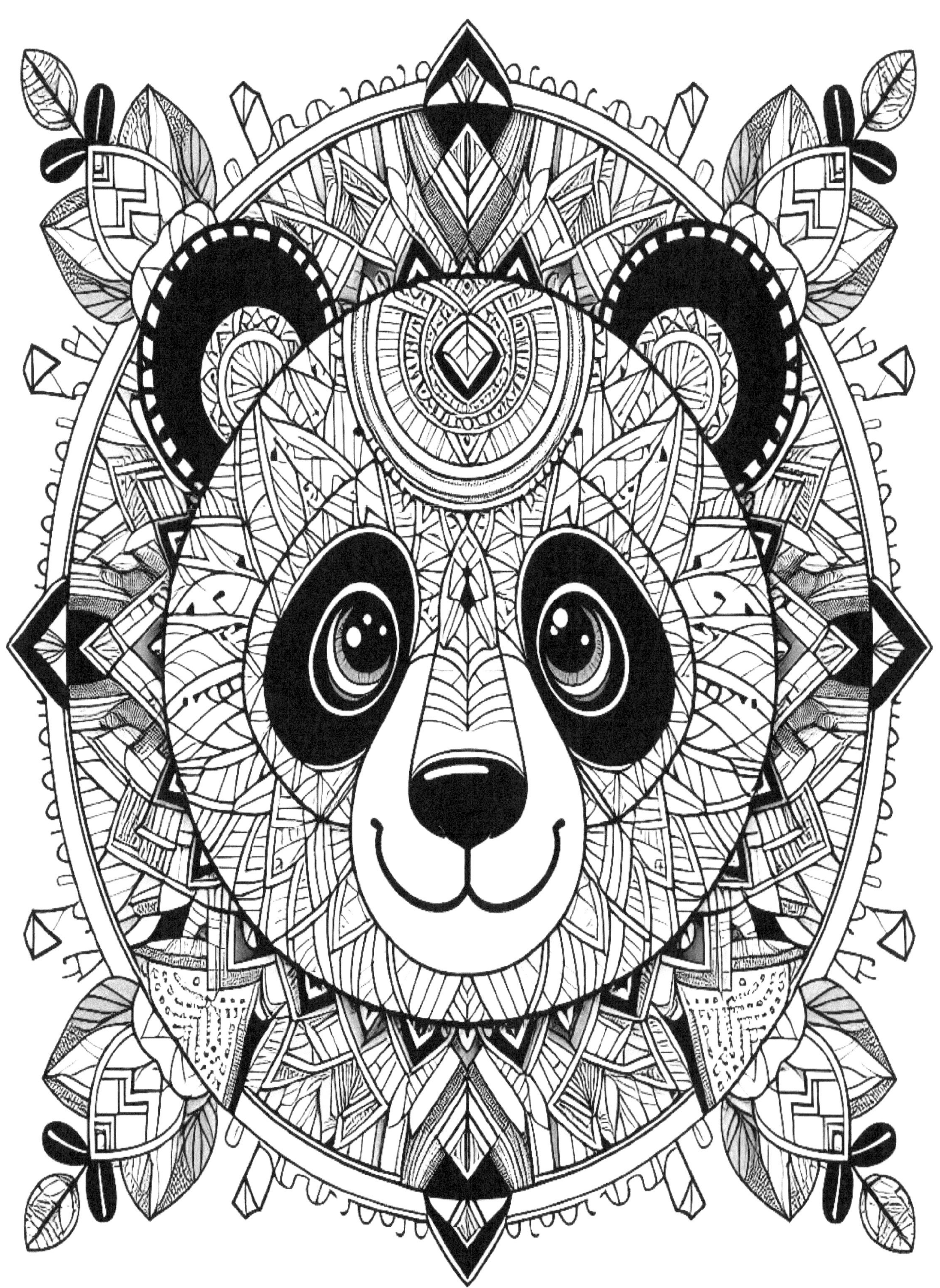

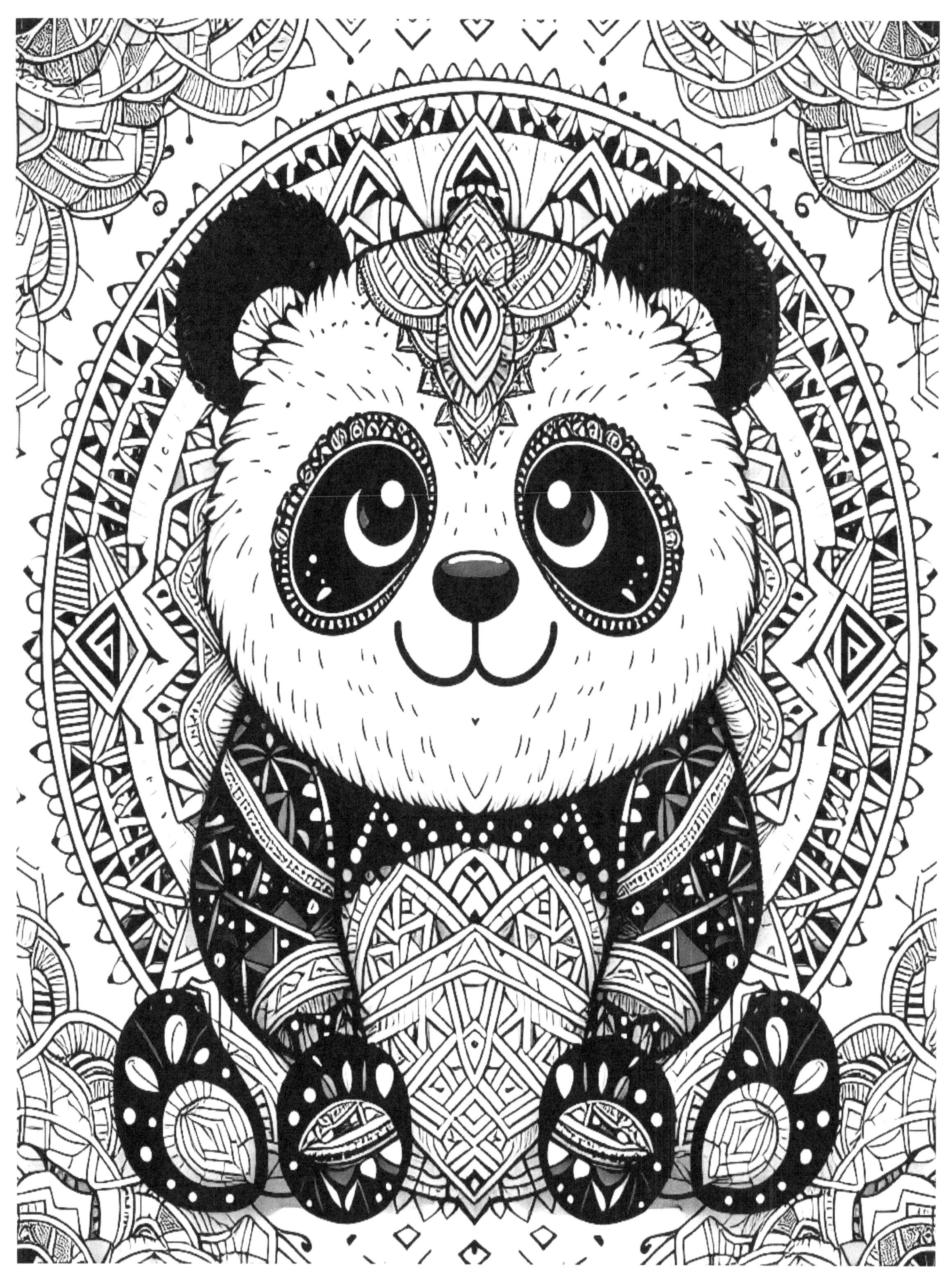

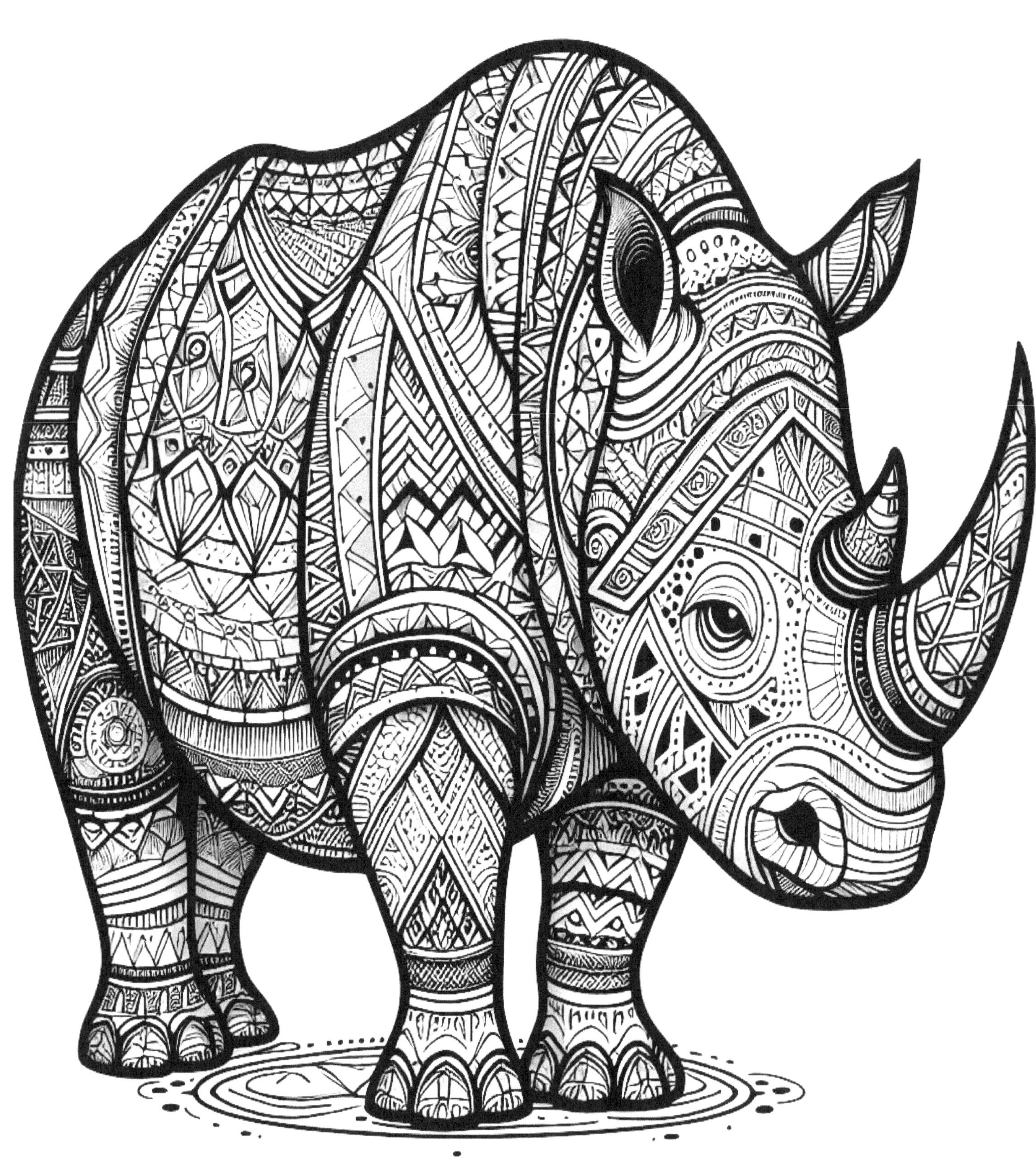

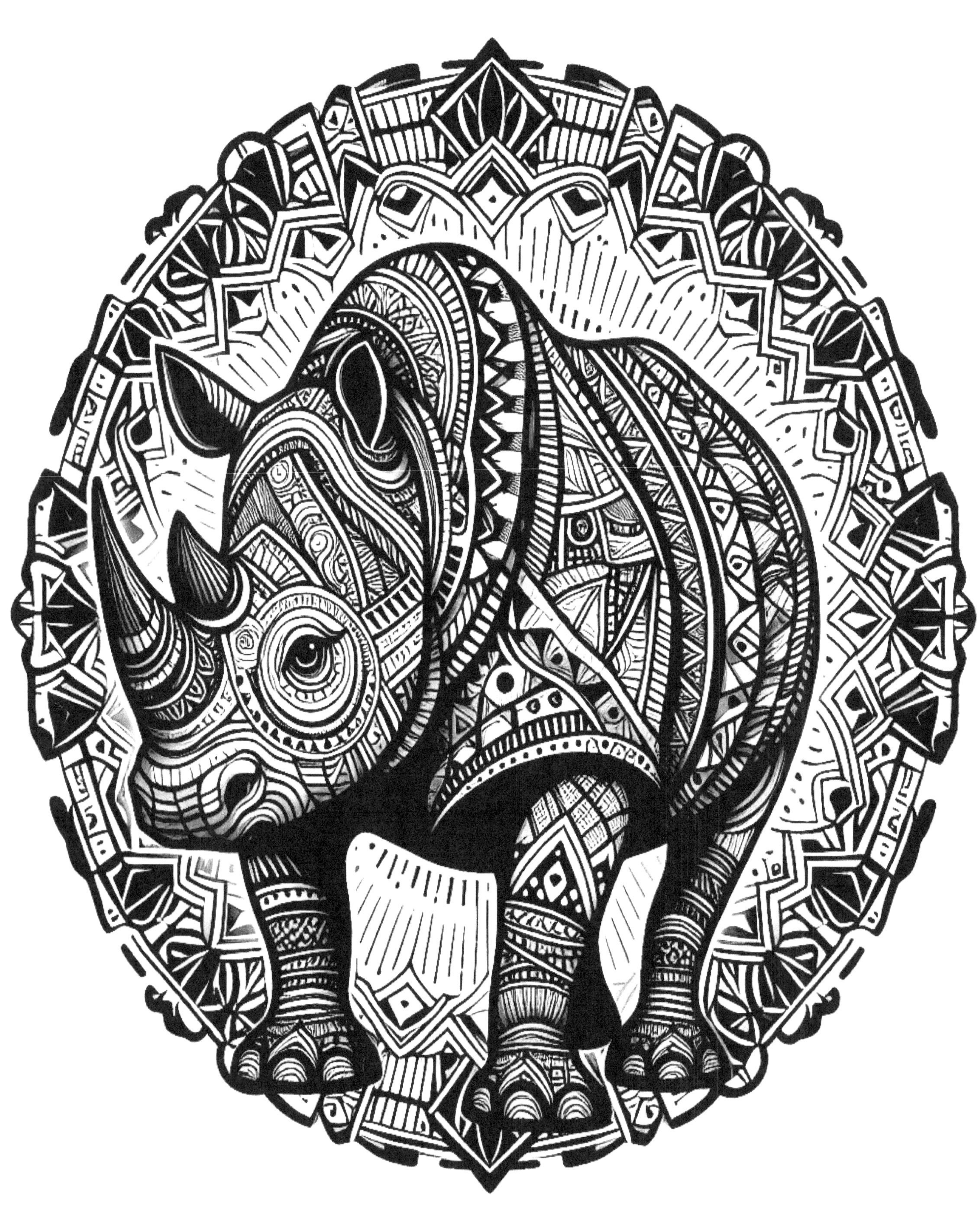

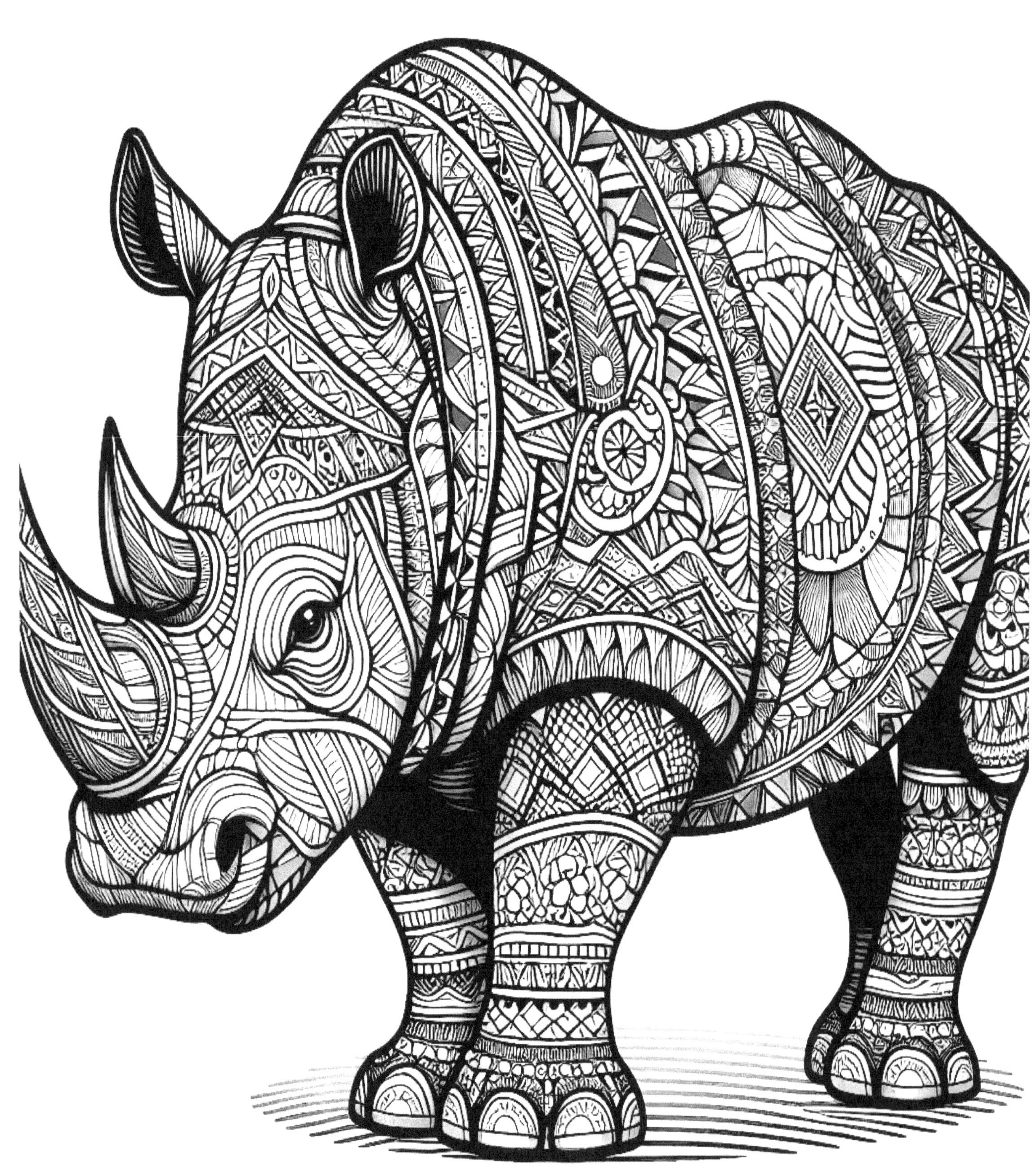

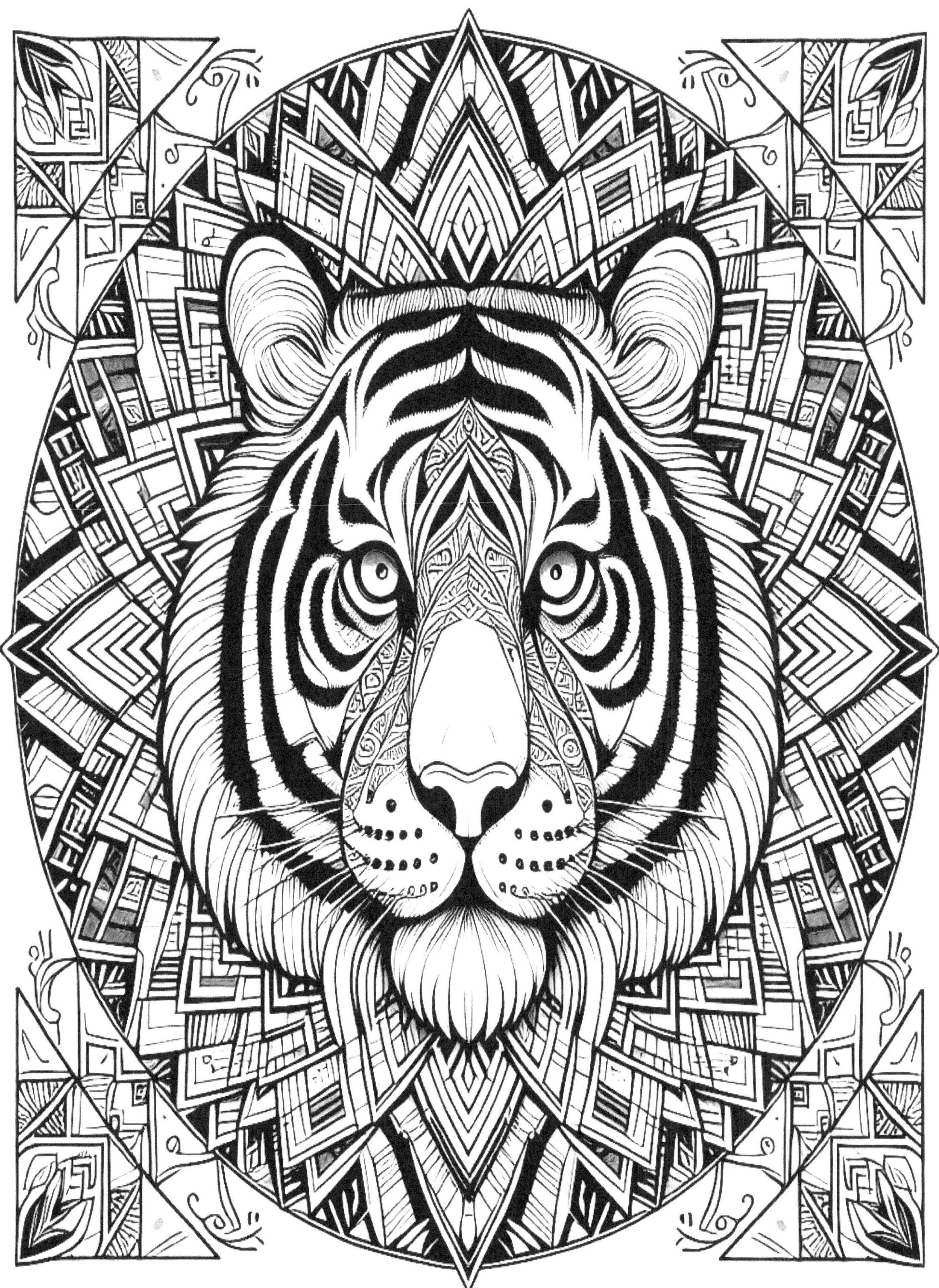

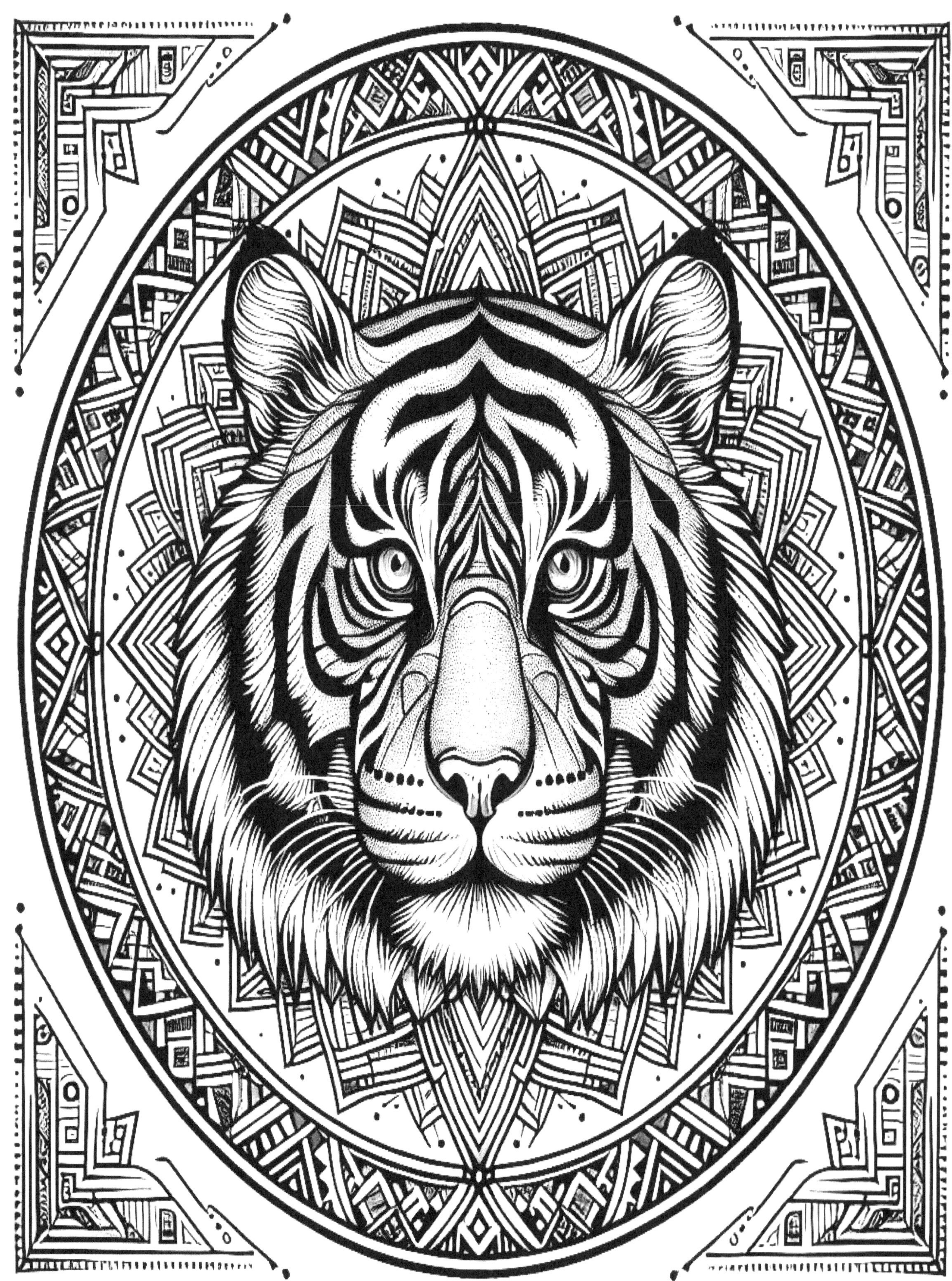

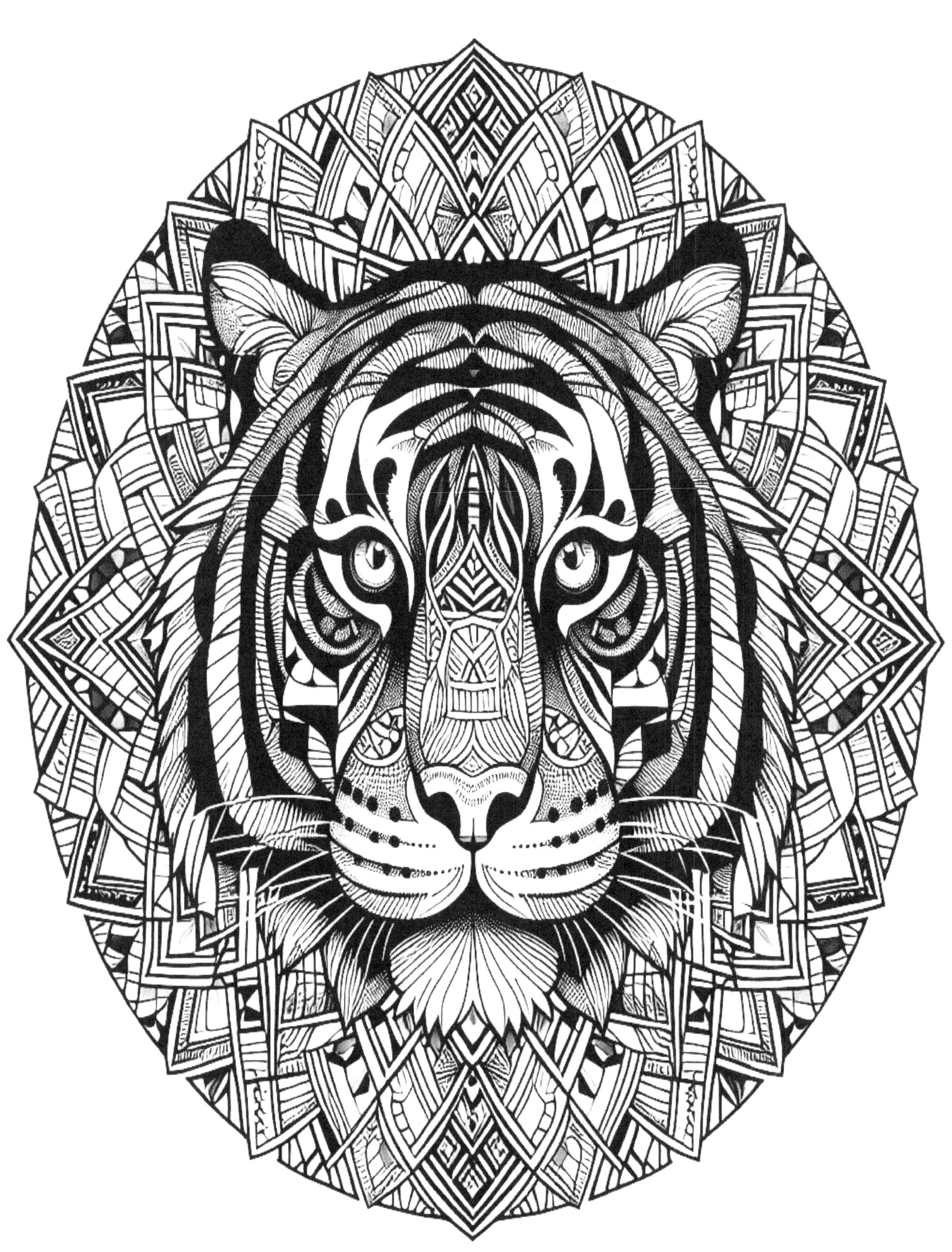

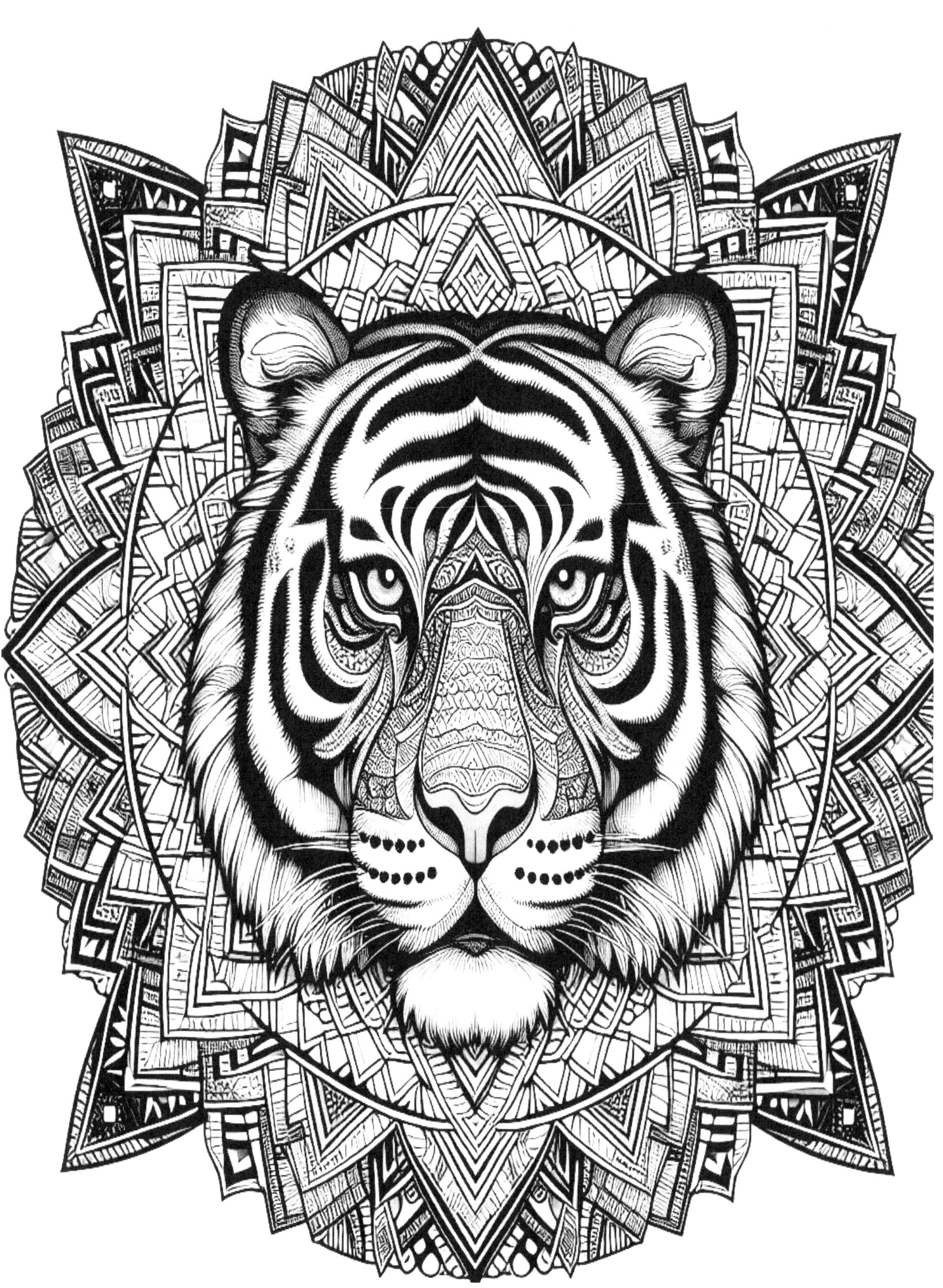

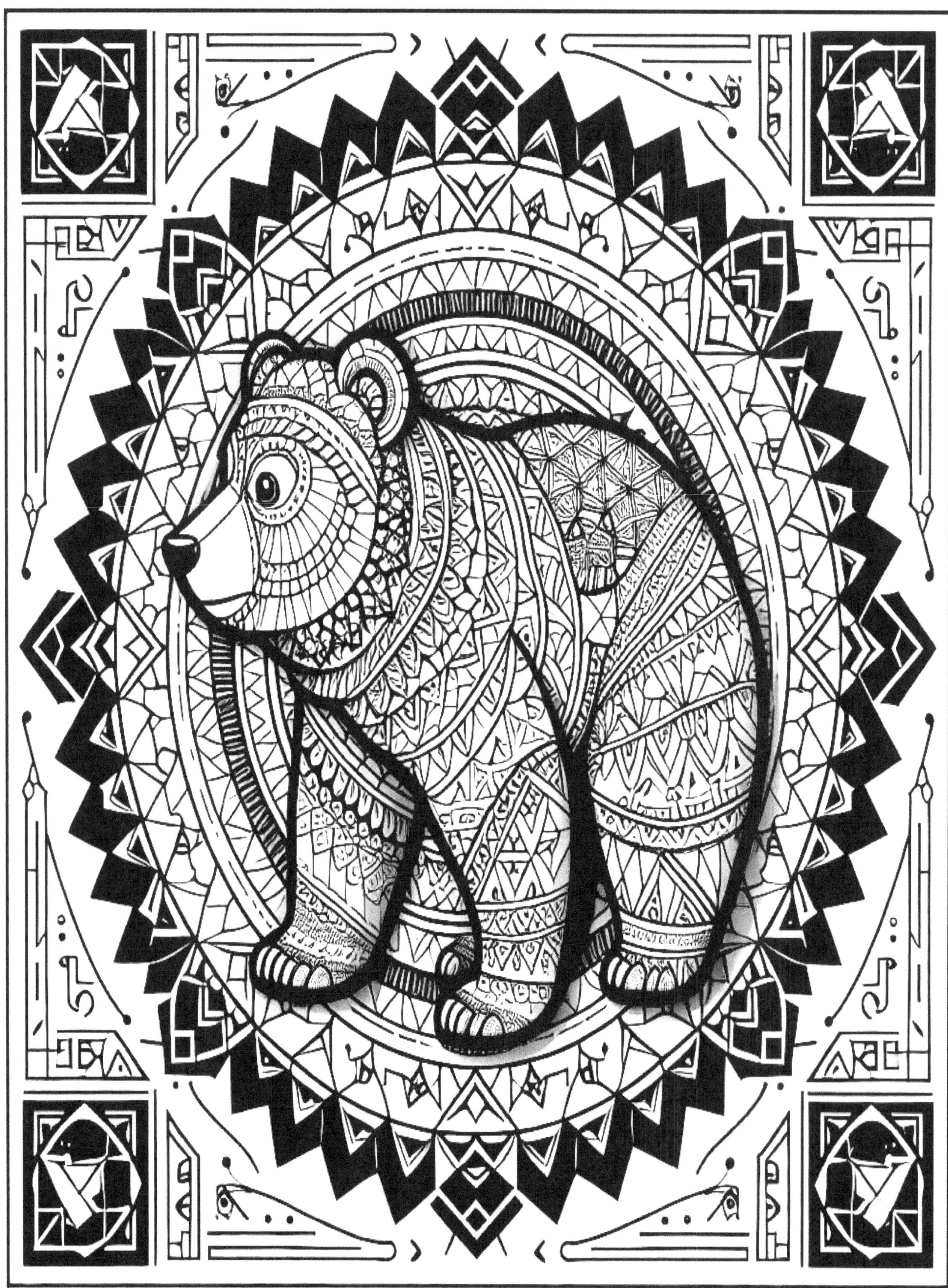

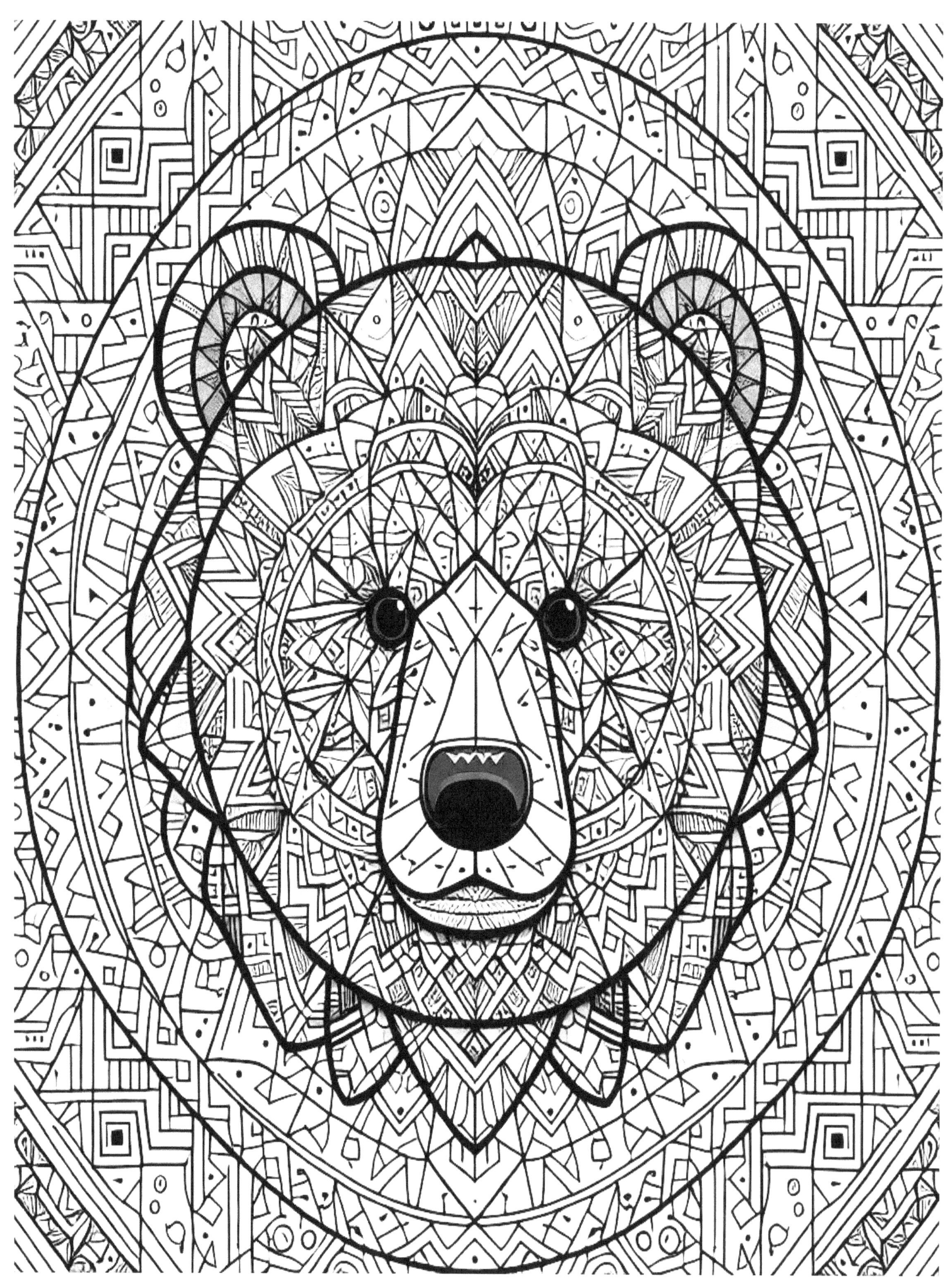

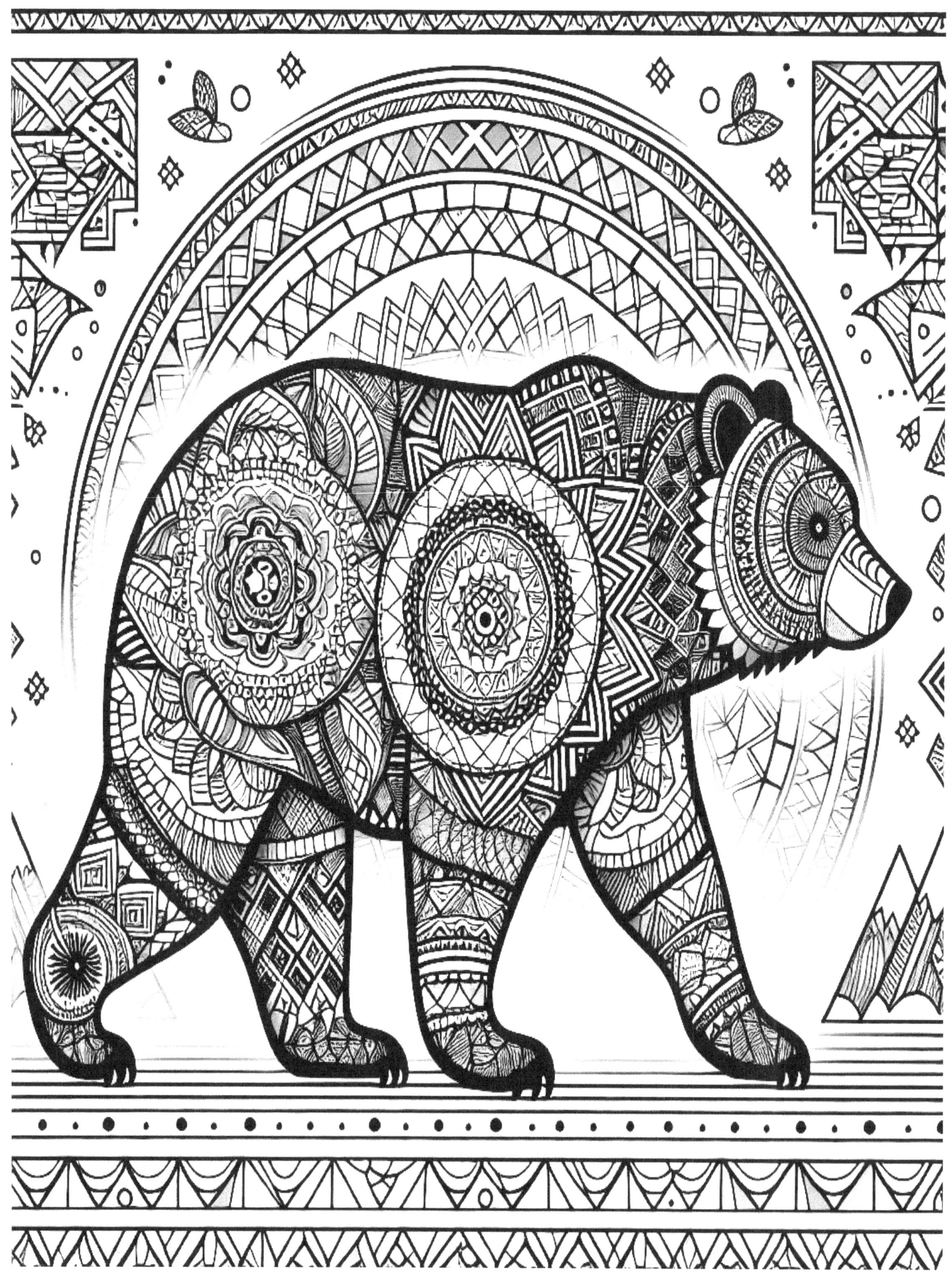

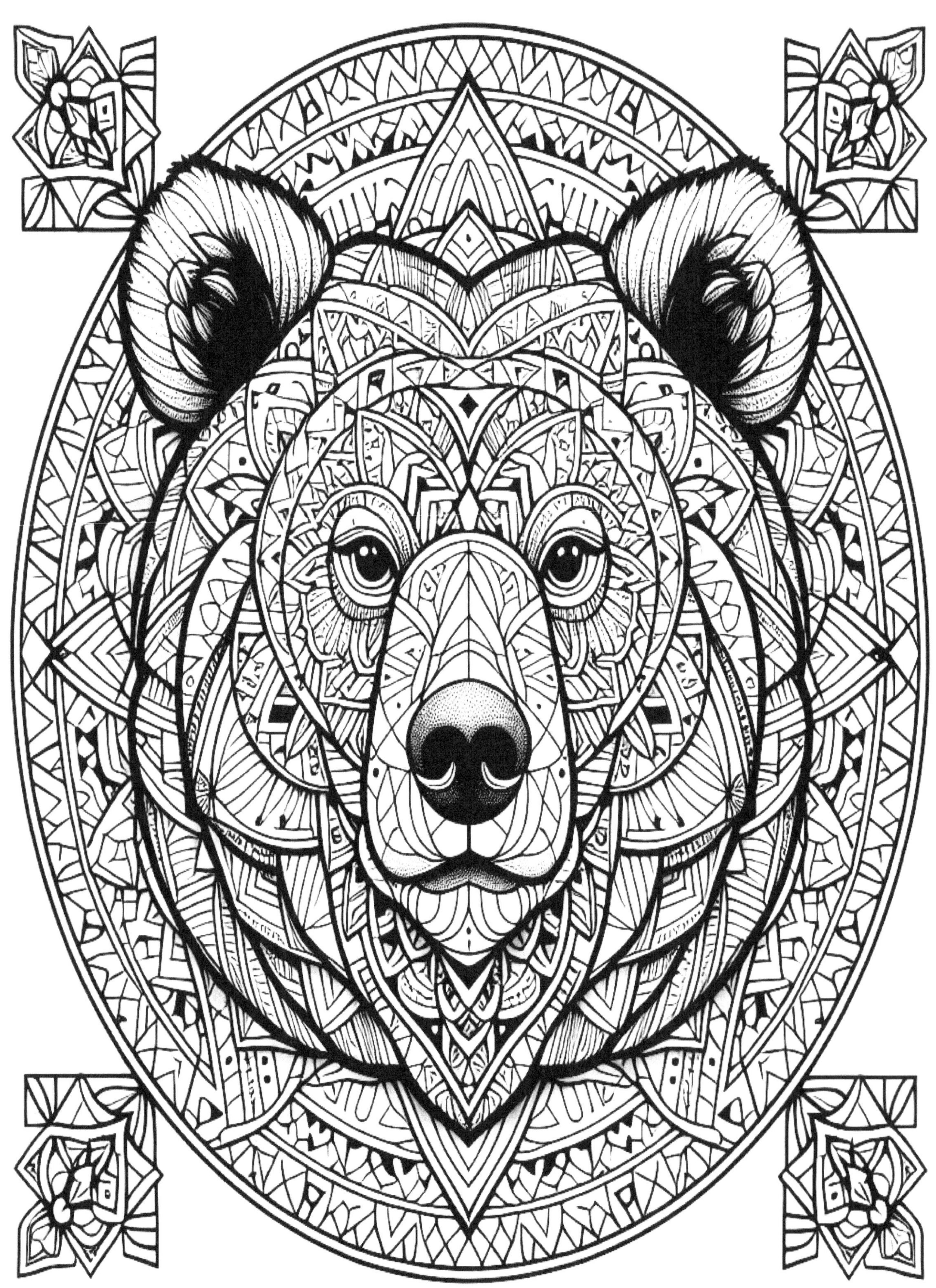

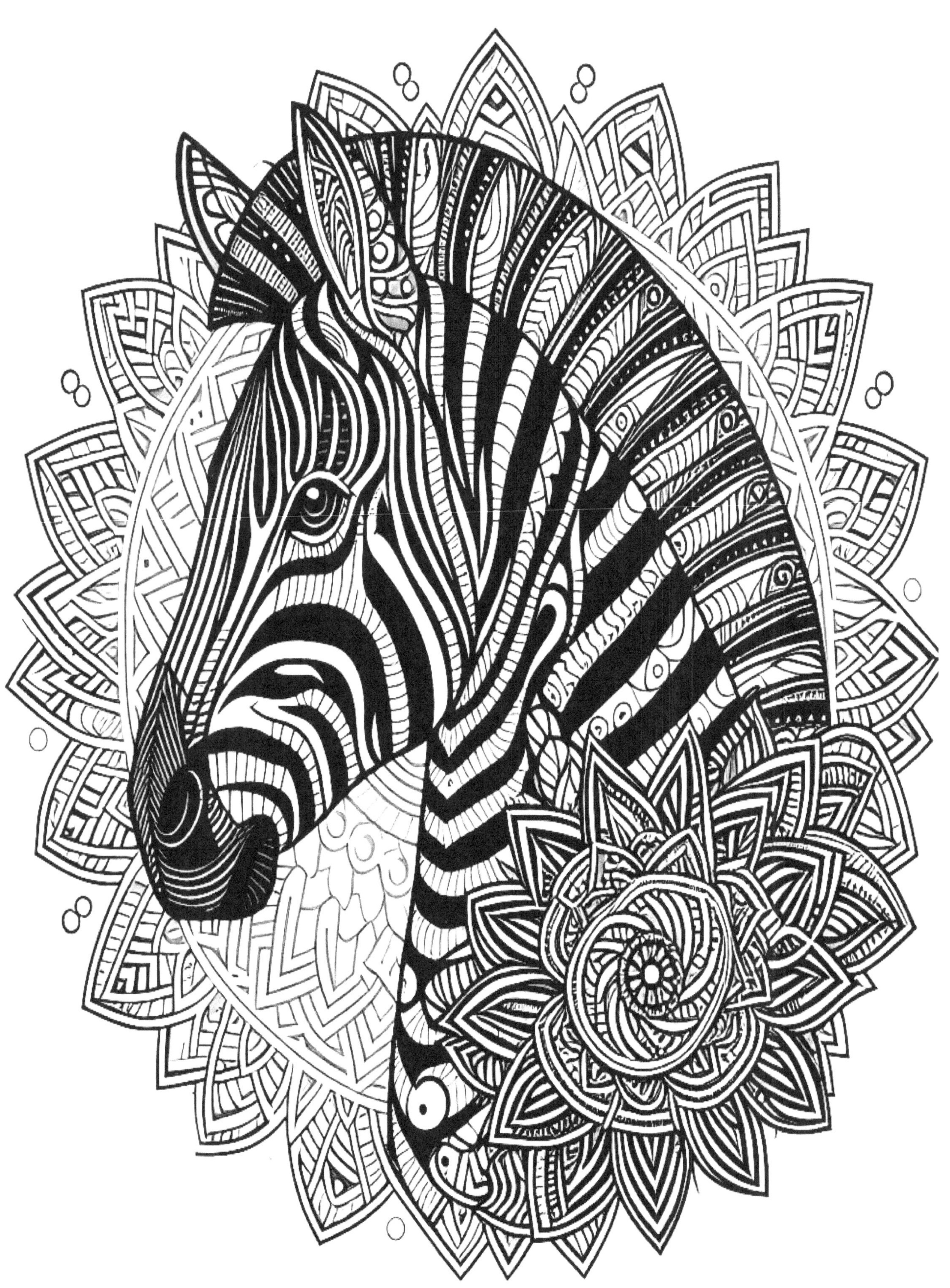

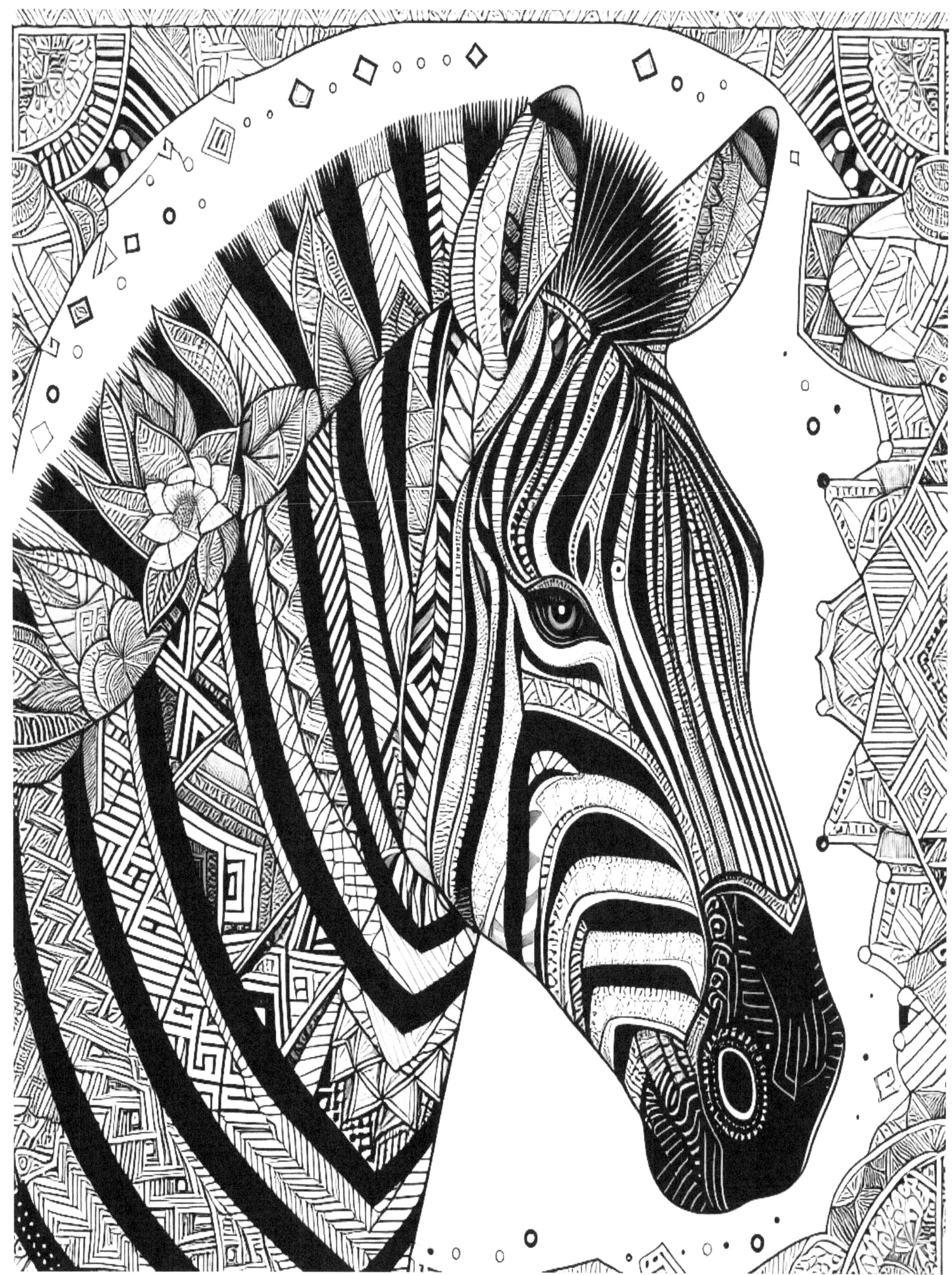

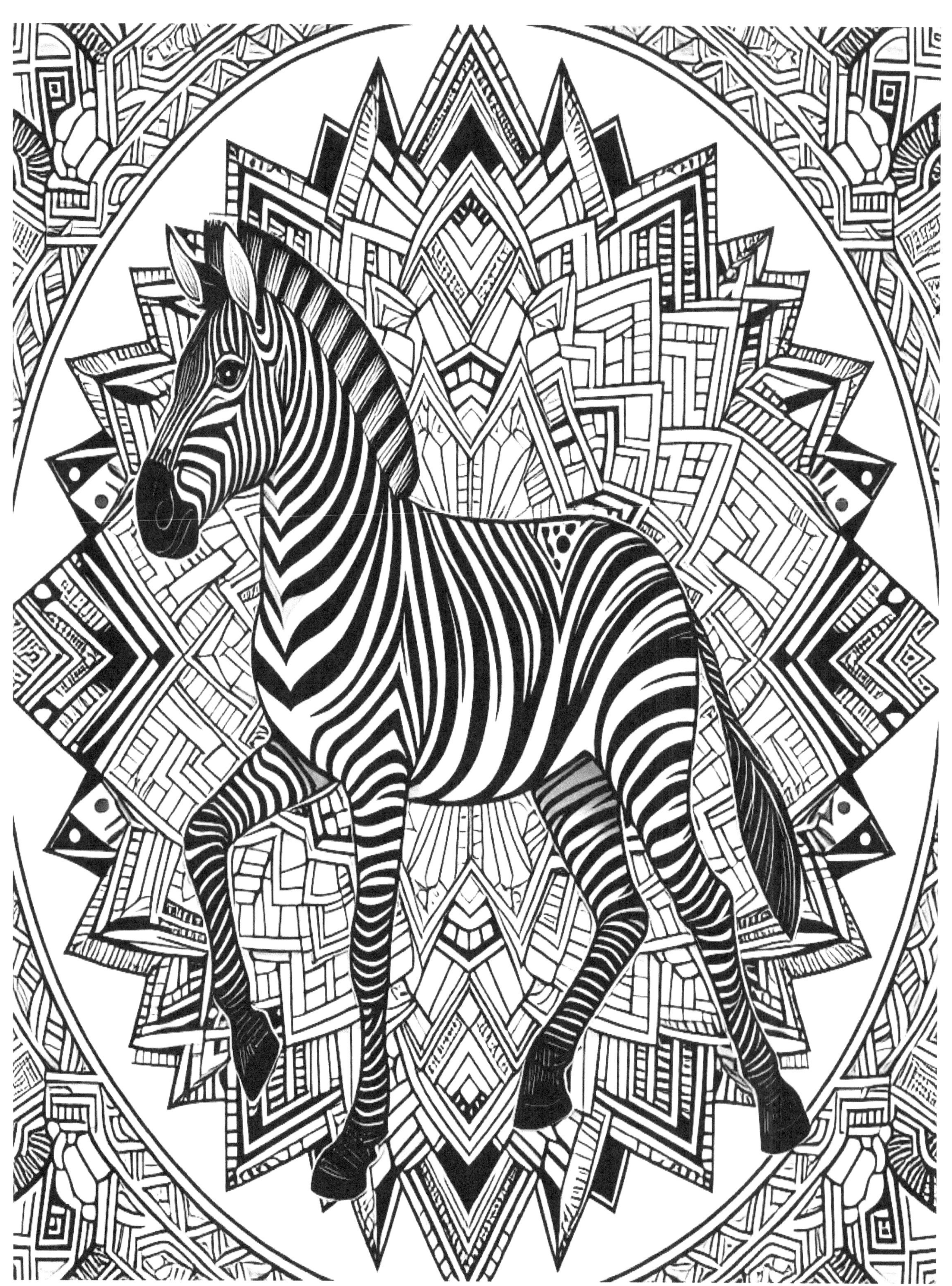

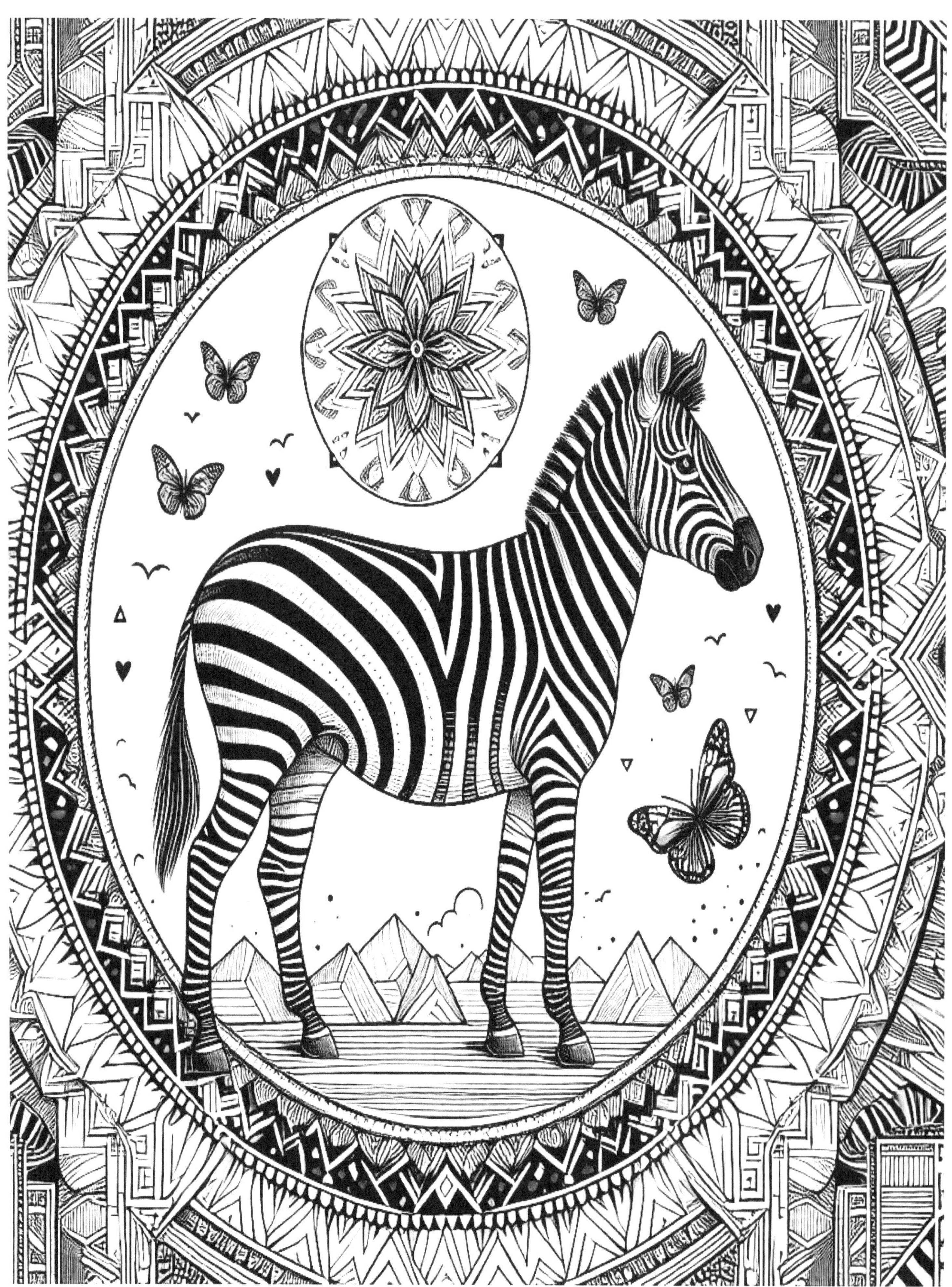